HOW *to*
MAKE MONEY
in
ALTERNATIVE INVESTMENTS

HUBERT BROMMA
LISA MOREN BROMMA

New York   Chicago   San Francisco   Lisbon   London
Madrid   Mexico City   Milan   New Delhi
San Juan   Seoul   Singapore   Sydney   Toronto

The *McGraw-Hill* Companies

Copyright © 2010 by The McGraw-Hill Companies, Inc. All rights reserved.
Printed in the United States of America. Except as permitted under the United
States Copyright Act of 1976, no part of this publication may be reproduced
or distributed in any form or by any means, or stored in a database or retrieval
system, without the prior written permission of the publisher.

1 2 3 4 5 6 7 8 9 0 DOC/DOC 0 1 6 5 4 3 2 1 0 9

ISBN 978-0-07-162377-3
MHID 0-07-162377-9

This publication is designed to provide accurate and authoritative information
in regard to the subject matter covered. It is sold with the understanding that
neither the author nor the publisher is engaged in rendering legal, accounting,
futures/securities trading, or other professional service. If legal advice or other
expert assistance is required, the services of a competent professional person
should be sought.

> —*From a Declaration of Principles jointly adopted by a Committee
> of the American Bar Association and a Committee of Publishers*

McGraw-Hill books are available at special quantity discounts to use as
premiums and sales promotions, or for use in corporate training programs. To
contact a representative please e-mail us at bulksales@mcgraw-hill.com.

This book is printed on acid-free paper.

Library of Congress Cataloging-in-Publication Data
Bromma, Hubert Franz-Josef.
  How to make money in alternative investments / by Hubert Bromma and Lisa
Moren Bromma.
    p. cm.
  ISBN 0-07-162377-9 (alk. paper)
  1. Investments. 2. Portfolio management. 3. Real estate investment. I. Bromma,
Lisa Moren. II. Title.
  HG4521.B678 2010
  332.63—dc22

                                                                    2009016403

CONTENTS

CHAPTER

INVESTOR SURVIVAL SKILLS FOR CHALLENGING TIMES
An Overview of Alternative Investing

H ave you lost money in the stock market? Who hasn't? Especially since the Dow Jones Industrial Average plunged 5,000 points and almost 40 percent in 2008. Has your home or other real estate dropped in value from the heyday of just a few years ago? Are you watching your retirement funds disappear, just when you're getting to an age when you'll need that money most, if you don't already?

If you're like many Americans, the answer to all these questions is unfortunately a horrifying *yes*. If you're wondering what you can do now, this book is for you because the stock market is not the only way to invest, and you don't need to limit yourself to traditional investments in stocks, bonds, and mutual funds. There are dozens of *alternative* investments that have proven to be profitable for us personally and for many of our clients. This book describes those investments and how you can determine if any are right for you and your financial portfolio, and how you can get started in each.

Why You Need This Book Now, More Than Ever

Wherever you go these days, you hear fear because, in recent months, people have been feeling the winds of change—and some of us are being blown away. Since the subprime mortgage crisis burst the real estate bubble, the number of foreclosures has skyrocketed, and housing prices have plunged nationwide. On Wall Street, major banks—including such industry leaders as Lehman Brothers Holdings Inc. and American International Group, Inc. (AIG)—have failed, causing a panic among all other banks. We're seeing consolidation among major banks nationwide and a tightening of credit.

As mentioned, the stock market went wild, though not in a good way: stocks plummeted 40 percent in value. That meant that the millions of Americans who were invested heavily in the market during this period lost 40 percent of their money, which had likely been earmarked for their kids' college education or for their own retirement. Major companies laid off thousands of people, causing unemployment to increase. The Big Three carmakers looked to the government for help in surviving their financial crises.

In response, retailers have been putting everything on sale. However, that's good news for consumers only in the very short term because we're facing deflation that will further stagger the U.S. economy. In fact, we're no longer in a market correction or even a recession; instead, the D word is being used as comparisons are being made between today's economy and the Great Depression of 1929.

That's a tough environment to face, and anyone who invests any amount of money is right to be worried. Fortunately, you don't have to tear out your hair or lose sleep; you just need to take control of your investments, and you should consider diversifying in ways that few financial planners will advise. We've been investing in alternative investments for 40 years, and we've done so successfully because we're willing to research nontraditional ways to invest. We have been making these investments without much outside professional advice—although we do extensive due diligence on all potential investments. We believe in the motto of a good friend who told us this many years ago:

Never allow others to vote on your money.

For those who wish this to be true, this book is for you.

TAKE CONTROL OF YOUR INVESTING: DON'T DELEGATE IT TO ANYONE ELSE

In the past, most people with busy lives listened to their financial planners. Now that many have lost a significant percentage of their portfolios, investors are exercising their own power and learning how to take control of their financial future with investments that they select, understand, and believe in. Now more than ever, whether you want to grow your portfolio with tax-deferred or non-tax-deferred investments or with tax-free or taxable investments, *you* must take control of how you invest and what you invest in. If you allow others to decide how you invest, you will never have the money you need to take care of yourself now and when you retire. By taking personal control of your investments, you can grow your net worth, and this book will help you because it offers a fresh perspective on investing.

Traditional investments like stocks, mutual funds, and bonds are obviously not as attractive as they once were—in just one brief two-month period alone in 2008, the Dow plunged 5,000 points. The good news is that while the values of traditional investments have been eroding, millions of people have had success investing directly in assets they know, understand, and can control. These people are growing their savings by investing in what we call *alternative investments*—oil and gas exploration, water and air rights, gold and silver, equipment leasing, car loans, private mortgages and loans, mobile homes for affordable housing, real estate (both in the United States and other countries), foreign currencies, bank start-ups, green investments such as wind and solar energy, and much more.

None of these are the traditional investments that people make through a stockbroker or financial professional. Instead, these investments are usually made by people on their own, which means that there is no third party trying to put them in an investment on which the financial professional makes a commission. Imagine that: Not only do the investors make these investments *directly*, but they also earn more profit because the cost of getting into and out of the investments is much less.

Every investor is unique, but all investors want to get ahead financially. Whether your money is in a tax-deferred account like an individual retirement account (IRA) or in some other type of account, whether you have $1,000 or $1 million, it is your right to choose how you want to invest that money. The choices we offer in this book are relevant to today's economy. Investing doesn't have to be limited to stocks, bonds, mutual funds, and real estate. There is a world of choices out there for investors who want more choices.

Our clients and readers are not expecting the Social Security check when they turn 65. They already anticipate that there might not be Social Security. That's why this book is so important—because it will describe many ways to make alternative profitable investments. In addition, it will dispel the myths surrounding alternative investing and give you the dos and don'ts for each investment type, so you can make informed choices.

WE'VE PROFITED FROM OUR ALTERNATIVE INVESTMENTS—AND YOU CAN TOO

We have had direct experience with most investment types, both traditional and alternative, including water rights, gas rights, oil rights, solar-powered homes, mobile homes, storage facilities, private loans to consumers and businesses, precious metals, and even cow and horse trailers. In the chapters that follow, we share stories—both positive and negative—from our own experience and that of others. We tell real stories from real people, some of whom had only a little cash to invest but were still able to grow their wealth by making investments that they researched and understood. This book will help you invest in areas where *you* see potential, and it will give you the financial freedom of having a great many investment choices and not having to depend on a third party's recommendations.

So how did we get started in alternative investing? Both of us got started back in the late 1970s, though in different ways. Lisa got started in alternative investing through real estate, at first on a personal level but then branching out to many more types of real estate–based investments and other alternative investments. In 1978, Lisa was in her twenties and single and had moved to Florida with her two young children. She had never owned property before, but she decided that she would be better off owning property than renting. So she figured out a way to buy a home with only a $1,000 down payment, and she convinced the seller to finance the sale for her. The seller made a hard-money loan to Lisa of $39,000 at 12½ percent interest for 30 years. This arrangement was great for Lisa, because she wouldn't have been able to get a mortgage from a bank since she had no credit at that time. She lived in the house with her family for five years and then sold it for just under $44,000, realizing a profit of $4,000. Lisa then took that profit and bought another piece of real estate.

In the early 1980s, Lisa bought her first rental property. Over the next 30 years, she bought and sold many other properties—some for her family to live in and others for rental and resale—in various regions of the United States and in other countries. These investments have provided great ongoing cash flow (which we'll describe in detail in Chapter 7). In addition, she began diversifying her investments with other alternatives. For example, Lisa has made private loans to others who have invested in real estate (which we'll describe in Chapter 2); she has invested in other businesses' accounts receivable (which we'll describe in Chapter 8); and she has invested in gold (which we'll describe in Chapter 3).

Hugh got started in 1979 while working as the general auditor for a multibank holding company in California. He learned that some of the bank's clients weren't investing their IRAs only in certificates of deposit (which was a popular way to invest before the mid-1980s' era of mutual funds). Instead of certificates of deposit (CDs), some of these clients were investing their IRAs in *real estate*. For example, two clients, who were former insurance agents, discovered that the insurance companies were involved in individual retirement annuities that allowed you to invest in pretty much *anything*.

Hugh was intrigued that people would invest in something other than a safe and secure investment like a Federal Deposit Insurance Corporation (FDIC)–insured CD. Even more intriguing was the fact that these clients were investing in land developments in the California desert and in tourist regions in Mexico. These land tract developments were earning huge amounts of money for the investors. Hugh decided that what was working for his clients might also work for him, and he started researching and making similar types of investments.

A few years later, Hugh left that bank and started a consulting practice specializing in bank operations and mergers and acquisitions. Since then, Hugh has personally invested successfully in many alternative investments such as gold bars and silver coins (which we'll describe in Chapter 3); offshore oil rigs in Louisiana, where he invested in $10,000 increments over a four-year period and earned 20 percent on those investments (which we'll describe in Chapter 4); and real estate (which we'll describe in Chapter 7).

In 1992, Hugh founded Entrust Administration and The Entrust Group, whose clients choose how and where they want to invest their retirement accounts through a wide array of tax-deferred or tax-free investment options (including all those described in this book). Over the past 30 years, Hugh has helped his clients invest not only in the real estate deals that originally spawned his interest in alternative investments but also in many other vehicles (which we'll introduce you to later in this chapter). As the CEO of The Entrust Group, Hugh administers more than $3 billion in retirement money, and more than 40 percent of the company's 50,000 clients invest in alternative, nontraditional investments.

One nice thing about alternative investing is that once you've purchased the investment (whether it's real estate, a bank start-up, or a business), it will pay you on a monthly, quarterly, or annual basis, depending on the way you structure the paperwork. So you don't have to worry about marketplace fluctuations that create openings for the federal government to get involved by way of imposing regulations. That independence is one reason investors like to utilize alternative investments as a part of their investment strategy.

The Differences between Traditional and Alternative Investments

There are essentially three differences between traditional and alternative investments:

1. Alternative investments are generally not publicly traded. In the stock and bond markets, some sort of government or public action is involved. With an alternative investment, you are making that investment *directly*. You're not going to see it traded on the stock exchange nor are you going to see it being held or governed by a federal entity.

2. Alternative investors have a greater degree of hands-on involvement with their particular investments. They do some or all of the research, and they make their own decisions.

3. Alternative investors don't rely on a third-party opinion—for example, the opinion of a financial planner, broker, or advisor—to make their final investing decisions. Instead, they make their decisions and their investments *on their own.*

If you're interested in controlling your income and cash flow, if you want to take advantage of available tax enhancements or sheltering, if you want to capitalize on appreciation, and if you want to invest in your own way, then you are the perfect investor for the alternatives described in this book.

WHAT THIS BOOK *WON'T* TELL YOU

Of course, all of these alternatives come with their own associated risks and rewards. Nothing is easy in life. If you want to just have your money guaranteed for the rest of your life, leave it in a savings account with your bank—as long as it's in some bank that you feel is never going to go under.

In life, there's always a certain amount of gamble. It is not our job to make recommendations. It's our job to tell you about successful individuals who've utilized different types of alternative investment strategies to become successful in what they do. And that is what we're doing in this book: sharing with you how to make alternative investments.

NONTRADITIONAL WAYS TO INVEST YOUR MONEY—AND MAKE A PROFIT

So what are some of these alternative investments we're talking about? There are dozens, and we'll tell you true stories from real people to illustrate each type of investment that we describe.

In Chapter 2 on private lending, we show you how to lend money to other people, and how to do it safely and profitably. For example, Bill is an investor in Houston who makes private loans of about $50,000 every year at 12½ percent interest. The term of the loan is for only one year, with a guaranteed three-month return. Bill is an attorney, so if the person he lends money to doesn't pay him back, he will find a way to foreclose on whatever the person has— whether it's a home, a car, a boat, or any other type of real property—so he feels comfortable in making this type of investment. Of course, this type of private unsecured lending is not for everyone, but it works for Bill. He started years ago by investing $50,000 per loan, and he tries to do one every three months. By doing that, he has grown $200,000 in savings into more than $1 million.

In Chapter 3 on investing in precious metals, we give examples on how to invest in gold, silver, platinum, and titanium—both in the actual physical metals as well as in certificates that represent ownership. Of course, precious metals are also traded over the counter on the stock exchanges, and there are also gold mutual funds and mutual funds secured by other precious metals. But we consider precious metals to also be an alternative investment because many individual investors are utilizing commodities as mattress money. They believe that the economy will continue to worsen and that gold especially will be the currency of choice.

For example, Michael is a gold trader. He's been trading gold for the last 25 years very, very successfully. He started out with a relatively small interest: He bought $10,000 worth of gold in the form of certificates. These certificates are not publicly traded; instead, he buys them directly, as an individual, from the Perth Mint. The certificates are secured by the government of Australia, so if the Perth Mint defaults on the certificates, the Australian government will step in. That makes Michael feel very secure in this type of alternative investment. And Michael has parlayed his original $10,000 gold purchase into well over $100,000 by consistently buying and selling these gold certificates.

In Chapter 4 on investing in natural resources, we describe how people we know have invested in gas rights, oil rights, and water rights. For example, we know someone who invested $50,000 in water rights on land in Wyoming and received a return of several million dollars; another client invested $10,000 through a water rights broker and has quadrupled her money in only four years. We'll tell these and other stories in detail in Chapter 4, and we'll describe what you need to know to evaluate whether such investments are right for *you*.

In Chapter 5 on socially responsible green investing, we delve into how to invest in solar energy, wind power, and marine wave power, like Kathleen, who is an active investor in green communities. In this type of investment situation, an entire community is being built by financing fractional shares of the development. You would start out with, say, $100,000, and you would be investing in the actual community development. In Kathleen's investment, the developers are building green housing and green common areas and facilities, and they are using only solar power for the utilities. Kathleen's investment may have a three- to five-year payout by the time the community is secured, but she feels like she's doing something great for the environment. Her money will not be working at any particular interest rate at the moment, but she's counting on the appreciation potential in the long term, and she feels great that her $100,000 investment is green. Her investment is secured by the actual developer, but it's secured in such a fashion that she's taking an interest only in that community. She doesn't really own any real estate. We'll show you how to find these opportunities and how to evaluate whether they're right for you.

In Chapter 6 on international investing, we describe how to make currency, bond, and other investments on the foreign exchange market—that is, the forex. We'll also show you how to buy real estate internationally. Many people are getting into foreign investments—not only real estate but also foreign CDs from foreign banks. Banks all over the country advertise foreign investments for their clients for wealth management. We'll show you how to do this safely and wisely.

In Chapter 7 on investing in real estate, we tell you how you can still make money in the real estate market despite the downward spiral of property values. In real estate, you make money when you *buy*, and it's a buyer's market: Everything is on sale! You just have to know what to look for to invest profitably. We look at foreclosures—buying, financing, and what to look out for. There are also auctions, probates, even storage facilities for people to stash all their things.

We describe how to invest in real estate tax liens, which are the delinquent taxes that city and county governments need to pay for fire and police departments and other types of ongoing monthly expenses. As we all know, there are a lot of foreclosures right now, and those homeowners not only defaulted on their mortgages but also on their property taxes. The number of these tax defaults is so high that cities and counties are in trouble financially. Many financially strapped cities and counties are auctioning off these liens for delinquent taxes. This means that you can buy into a tax lien or a tax deed and get a good return on that investment that is paid by the county or city.

In Chapter 8 on investing in business-to-business cash flows, we discuss how to invest in banks and other start-up companies. For example, we know several investors who buy car paper. Ken routinely makes this type of investment. He "floor plans," meaning that he puts up the money so that a car dealer can go to auto auctions and buy cars at wholesale. While the cars sit on the lot unsold, Ken receives interest on the money he invested. Every time a dealer sells one, Ken gets paid off. Ken's investments are secured by the cars, and he keeps the titles until they sell. Only when he gets paid off does he release the titles. The dealers win because their borrowing costs are not as high as they would be from a bank, and Ken wins because he can drive by his investments any time he wants to.

We also tell you how Lisa has invested in bank start-ups, and how other investors we know have invested in dairy cows, where the cow contracts are secured by the dairy creamery. Does this make a good investment? After describing what you need to know, you can decide for yourself if that's the right investment for you. That's what this book is about: giving you informative and real case studies to help you think about the options for expanding your wealth.

In Chapter 9 on making alternative investments through your IRA or 401(k), we describe how to grow wealth with your retirement funds. Of special importance is the tax law that takes effect in 2010. In that year, we all have the ability to convert from a tax-deferred retirement plan to a tax-free plan, regardless of income. We'll show how you can do this—and why everyone who has an IRA should be doing this!

Finally, in Chapter 10, we tell you how to get started in the alternative investments of your choice. Because it *is* your choice that's important: Don't let someone else decide how and where you should invest your hard-earned money. No one cares more about your money than you do. Is alternative investing more work? Yes, it can be more work. But is there more reward? Absolutely, because you're controlling your own financial future, and you're not at the mercy of the government, a stockbroker, or the stock and bond markets.

As investors and owners of our own companies, we have found that when we take the time to learn about a new potential investment, we get a higher return than a financial professional would, and we come to feel comfortable with our investment choices. We have discovered a world of choices of nontraditional assets that we can take control of.

We're assuming that if you want to take control of your financial life, you have a brain and you're willing and able to do a little bit of work. That effort will go a long way in helping you realize your financial dream. Read on as we explore each individual type of investment that we feel is up and coming, that's relevant to today's times, and that you can capitalize on. With a little due diligence and know-how, initiative, and confidence, you can invest in alternative investments and realize great returns. We're not going to tell you what to do, because you need to make your financial and investing decisions for yourself. However, we will share with you strategies that we, and people we know, have utilized to make better returns on our money. Otherwise, what's the point of investing outside of a traditional market?

In other words, utilizing alternative investments gives you complete flexibility and makes you the ultimate investor. Do you want to keep some of your portfolio in traditional investments? If so, that's great. We're not suggesting that you divert everything out of your traditional investments and invest in alternative investments. What we're suggesting is this: Don't be caught with your pants down. Instead, utilize your abilities and opportunities to invest in these different types of cash flows and to grow your net worth.

Many of our clients have been asking for a how-to guide for a broad scope of investment opportunities. This book is our response to those requests. It is intended to help you, as an investor, determine if a particular investment is right for you. We make no investment recommendations, and we offer no investment advice. Instead, our goal is to educate you to make informed, common sense decisions that *you* are comfortable with. We show you how to invest without getting burned, so you'll know your options before you invest. We offer numerous case studies from real clients and from our own personal investing experience to show you how to take your investing to the next level, no matter how much money you start with today. Follow these steps, earn while you learn, and grow rich!

So turn the page and start reading about how other people have made money by diversifying beyond stocks, bonds, and mutual funds into a world of nontraditional, alternative investments. Let's get started!

CHAPTER

2

PRIVATE LENDING
Earning Interest on Your Money by Making Loans to Other People

Do you remember in the old Popeye cartoons how Popeye's friend Wimpy was forever saying to him, "I'll gladly pay you Tuesday for a hamburger today"? That's essentially what private lending is: If you lend me money today, you should get something in return, right?

Private lending has evolved into quite an industry due to the problems that have developed in our economy because of subprime lending, mortgage foreclosures, banks that have folded or have been acquired by others, and mortgage brokers who are now out of business. People are spinning their wheels looking for loans.

In this chapter, we start with some history of private lending and Other People's Money (or OPM), and then we describe how private lending works today, with some real-world examples. We also share how to make private loans, whether you want to make loans via seller-financed mortgages, factoring, or lending to businesses. And, if you really don't want to do all that work, we tell you how you can simply tap into organizations that handle the loans for you using private people's funds.

So let's start with a little bit of background on private lending, also referred to as investing in paper.

What Private Lending Is—and What It's Not

In the old days, when businesses or individuals wanted to borrow money, they borrowed it from commercial banks or other traditional sources, such as credit unions or nonprofit financial institutions. The primary way people obtained loans was by borrowing money from a bank. Of course, some people also did crazy things, like racking up their credit cards all the way (which some people still do today) and paying those 18 to 20 percent interest rates every month on their minimum payments. Many people also refinanced their house and mortgage or got a line of credit against the refinancing on their house, so they would have the cash to do whatever they needed.

Of course, it's not only individuals who need money; businesses seek out money too. In the past, businesses usually had a line of credit, or they would go to their bank and borrow money. Businesses have also used *angel funds*, whereby they received loans from private investors who had large amounts of capital to lend to businesses that they believed would succeed and then pay them back with interest. The angels would also receive equity in the businesses in which they were investing. Businesses have also gotten loans from other types of commercial finance companies as well as received assistance through the Small Business Administration (SBA).

Today, of course, with the market what it is, finding money has become a challenge for both individuals and businesses. In addition to trying the "traditional" methods listed, some businesses now obtain loans by pledging their accounts receivable as collateral, an arrangement that is called *factoring*, which we discuss in more detail in Chapter 8.

So what is the best way to use Other People's Money? OPM refers to a type of loan in which the lender is a private individual—as opposed to a lending institution—who is using his or her own money to make loans. The lender makes such loans to help others—sometimes businesses and sometimes individuals—in situations in which they may have gotten behind in payments so that they can make up the back payments or for other financial reasons. By lending personal funds, the lender—that is, the investor—is accruing wealth in the form of interest. The lender is placing funds in alternative investments instead of or in addition to traditional investments such as mutual funds or money market accounts.

Borrowing and lending money have been around forever. Today, however, the rules have changed. The private lending arena is such that individual investors can go out and use their own cash to make a return greater than they would have if they had otherwise utilized or invested that money.

Before we go any further in this discussion, let's address the issue of loan sharking, because being a private lender is *not* the same as being a loan shark. Hard-money lenders are individuals who lend their money in either business-to-business loans or business-to-consumer loans. The loans come with fees and higher interest rates than the conventional market. In contrast, loan sharks charge exorbitant fees, they charge points, and they charge higher interest rates. Moreover, loan sharks usually make very short-term loans, and then they roll those loans and charge even *more* fees and points to the people who are borrowing money from them. In other words, loan sharks are typically taking advantage of people's financial problems. This is *not* what we're proposing in this book.

Instead, we want to illustrate how you, the investor, can place your cash in a loan that you feel is secure, whether you're making a private loan to a person or a business or you're acquiring a seller-financed loan. Whether the seller-financed loan is a loan secured by a piece of real estate or it's secured by a Subway restaurant franchise, you can actually utilize your money for a higher return when it's secured by some sort of collateral. Unsecured loans are entirely different and very risky, and they are the type of loans that loan sharks typically make. Obviously, when someone makes a loan at 30 percent interest, and it's unsecured by any type of collateral, there is risk. If you do this type of investing, you are basically "rolling the dice," with a 50-50 chance of getting repaid.

We strongly encourage caution. You should not consider lending your money at higher than the usury rate limit, because you can get yourself in trouble. Many states are proposing regulations that protect the consumer (not the investor) from unconventional lending practices.

Moreover, the only people who are typically interested in borrowing this way are fairly desperate. For example, we know someone—we'll call him Dan—who has a business in North Carolina. Dan has a tax problem: He failed to withhold payroll taxes on his employees. The IRS is threatening to garnish his wages, so Dan needs money quickly. He doesn't have any collateral. He can borrow money from a loan shark, who wants to charge him 18½ percent interest per month. Is that Dan's only option? If nobody else is going to offer to lend him money, he doesn't really have any other choice because the IRS might close down his business. That's a terrible situation to be in, and we are not proposing that you, the private investor, get involved in any type of situation like that.

In contrast, when you make a private loan, you should be lending money to someone who has a good reason for the loan and who has a repayment system in place. You need to feel secure that you're going to get your money back. As a result of making the private loan, you are entitled to a higher-than-normal interest rate on your investment as compensation. The rate is negotiable.

MAKING PRIVATE LOANS TO INDIVIDUALS

What we propose is that ideally you look at private lending with security—that is, with some type of collateral. That security could be a multitude of different things.

There are different considerations if you're making a loan to a business than if you're making a loan to an individual. Below is a list of some of the information we feel you need to determine when you're considering making a loan to an individual:

1. What does the individual need the loan for?
2. If it's secured, what is it secured by—for example, a car, a boat, a plane, a house?

3. What is the value of what you are making the loan against? If the security is a property, what is the value of that property? If it's a car, what is it worth?
4. How long do you need to make the loan for?
5. At what interest rate should you be compensated?
6. Are you going to accrue the interest for some period of time?
7. How is this person going to pay you back: monthly, quarterly, annually?

Deciding whether or not you're going to accrue interest (question 6 above) is an important question for investors, because some investors don't necessarily want to receive the cash on a regular basis. Many investors prefer to defer the interest on the loan they've made (and of course, they'll pay the taxes as the interest on the loan is repaid in full). So you need to consider your own personal situation and preferences before you make any type of loan.

Many investors make private loans from their IRA funds because the interest on those loans comes back into the IRA account, which is tax deferred. If investors make private loans from their Roth IRA funds, the interest flows into the Roth tax free. In our own client base at Entrust, we see a lot of individuals utilizing their IRA funds to make private loans (we cover more about this in Chapter 9).

Making Private Loans to Businesses

If you're making a loan to a business, the same questions as for individuals apply. In addition, you should first review the business plan of the particular business you're thinking of lending to so that you understand all of the following:

- What does the business owner do?
- What is the nature of the business?
- What does the business need money for?
- How will the loan be secured and repaid?

This might sound simple and obvious, but you wouldn't believe how many investors don't *really* understand the nature of the business that they are lending money to.

If you're making a loan to a business for direct infusion into the business itself, look at the business owners' financial plan and their profit-and-loss (P&L) statements for at least the last two to three fiscal years, if they've been in business that long. Also, keep in mind that 90 percent of businesses fail in the first five years, so the longer the business has been in existence, the better off you are if you're considering investing because the business needs a cash infusion. A company that has been doing business for more than five years is a relatively stable business and a less risky investment.

If you as a private investor are considering lending money to a business owner who has run into a cash flow problem (like Dan with his delinquent IRS payments or a situation in which the business owner has to make payroll immediately), and the loan is the only way the owner can get the money needed, you must do the necessary due diligence to protect yourself. You might also want to look at some accounting statements and cash flow balances that the business has so that you feel comfortable in the loan you are making.

Here's an example. Ray had a restaurant that he bought six months ago from another individual. He decided that he wanted to expand the space in his restaurant because there wasn't enough seating and it was impacting his business and the potential for more profit. He optioned adjacent property to expand, but he needed to come up with the cash so he could build out the space. Ray went to an investor, Jane, and he said to her, "I need $150,000, and I'm willing to put up some collateral for the loan. The bank won't lend me any more money because I have tapped out my equity on the existing loan. I tried the SBA to see if I could get an additional loan, but they haven't gotten back to me yet. I really believe in my business plan, and I want to get started now."

Ray was willing to put up some of his restaurant equipment as collateral. He calculated that he had about $200,000 worth of restaurant equipment. Jane looked at his place and said, "Let me see your business plan." His business plan was solid: Ray showed that if he could expand his business utilizing Jane's cash, he would be able to grow his restaurant because there would be more seating available, and he would be able to serve more customers. He had a business plan that Jane could look at, and that plan clearly told her what Ray needed the money for. Jane believed Ray was committed and would repay the loan. He had some security in the restaurant equipment, which could be appraised so that she would have an objective third-party value of the collateral. That's the first thing investors should do if they're looking to lend money to a business: find out what the money is for, what the business plan is, and what the business owner can offer as security in case he or she defaults on the loan.

The next thing you should do if you're considering lending money to a business is determine how you will get paid back. What is your return on this investment? Is there the potential for a piece of the business itself as compensation for making the loan? For example, in the case of Ray's restaurant, could you actually make a profit from his increased business revenue and improvements to the restaurant addition? The saying that "everything in life is negotiable" applies here. Negotiating between the person who needs the money and you, the investor, should always happen. Always remember, as the investor, that cash is king and you are in control of the situation. As long as you are negotiating an honest, fair structure, you help solve the problem, and you get the opportunity to invest your cash at interest rates that are higher than today's average bank rates.

For example, Jane could go back to Ray and say, "Okay, I will give you the $150,000, with the following conditions: I want to be paid back over the next year at 10 percent interest. I also want 5 percent of the profits you make in year two, based on an audited financial statement by a CPA in good standing." She further explains the risk that she has (should he not pay back) and that she feels this risk warrants fair compensation to her for making him the loan. Of course, Jane (a smart investor) puts her offer in writing. Now the ball's back in Ray's court. But, because Jane has the cash, she's in the driver's seat. Ray and Jane come to an agreement, and Jane makes the loan subject to review of the financials and appraisal. This type of private lending is done quite frequently, especially for small business owners who need short-term money.

In private lending, everything is negotiable: the exit strategy of when you're going to get paid back, your return on that investment, and how you're going to be paid, whether it's monthly, quarterly, or you're going to let that money ride until the end of the year. These are all negotiable items that you, the investor, must feel comfortable with before you make the loan.

If Ray doesn't pay Jane back, she can seize his business. She gets the inventory as well as all the restaurant equipment. And if Jane doesn't want to own a restaurant, she can turn around and sell it. So that's another consideration: You need to think about what you're going to do with this collateral if you end up owning it. Are you comfortable with the possibility of owning that business?

Another critical consideration is getting an attorney involved. If you don't already have an attorney, you need to find a business attorney, and yes, that will cost you money. But paying for an attorney's advice and work is worthwhile because you need to be protected. Ask your attorney to draw up the IOU, or the promissory note, as well as whatever collateralizing documents are involved, which in most cases is the Uniform Commercial Code Form 1 (UCC-1). The form is filed in the state where the business is located or incorporated.

Also, we strongly advise you to have *your* attorney draw up all the papers, rather than an attorney who is representing the person who wants to borrow money from you. The reason is that you know your attorney is representing you and your best interests. This protects you in the event that, for some reason, the business can't afford to pay you back. If that should happen, you need to immediately seize the business or whatever collateral has been put up as security for the loan. Although that's a worst-case scenario, you must plan for that because every private loan you make might not go smoothly. So it's very, very important to have an attorney draw up the loan documents for you.

Lending Money Using Real Estate as Collateral

As we've discussed so far, private lending doesn't deal only with consumers; it also deals with businesses, and it can even deal with certain types of small governments. Although the majority of investors who get involved in making private loans make loans to individuals, investors frequently make loans to small groups of property owners. The discussion that follows covers both situations: property owned by individuals and property owned by small groups.

Most of the real estate private loan situations concern individuals or small groups of people who have bought commercial property, such as small strip centers, apartment buildings, or storage facilities. Some of the people looking for loans may have a construction company, and some may have bought residential or mixed-use property. There are many different types of property that an individual or a small group of individuals can buy. When properties are owned by small groups of individuals, these partnerships or limited liability companies (LLCs) are always looking for investor dollars.

In this tough economy, more and more individuals and small groups—in partnerships or corporations—are seeking private money for residential, commercial, or land loans. Many types of loans are available—conventional, hard money, and private capital loans—and the terms of the loans are dictated on a case-by-case basis. The primary factors in choosing the type and terms of a loan are the nature of the project, who is borrowing the money, the borrower's credit scores, and other circumstances that pertain to the project or borrower.

For example, suppose 10 people are getting together and lending money so an apartment building can be purchased. The security is the apartment building itself, and the 10 owners of the building are going to put up some money and go to the bank to borrow the rest. This is a conventional loan. If the 10 owners cannot qualify for a loan, they have to go outside the traditional lending arena and work with private lenders. One or more investors could make a loan to the group secured by the building, or the 10 might shop for an unconventional private fund of money for their loan. Private lending comes in when an individual or a business cannot get conventional financing. In that case, the borrowers go to an individual investor to make that type of a loan, or to a company that's in the business of private lending. Generally, the security or lack of security determines what the interest rate of the loan will be and what the repayment period of time will be on that private loan.

We have seen private money offered on many types of loans, including mortgage loans, personal loans, and business loans. From cars to cows to water and solar energy (just to name a few), investors are "becoming the bank" with their own cash and growing their net worth with investments they researched and understood before they lent the money. Unlike the days when we depended on third parties to invest our money in GM and Ford stock, investors with cash are realizing that they need to take control of their financial future. Private lending is a great way for investors to jump into the cash flow industry. Our recommendation, if this type of investment interests you, is to start with low dollars and make sure you do your homework before you lend. Loans that are offered to borrowers after assessing their credit, terms, and other factors that we've discussed are loans you negotiated, and you are being rewarded with a higher return on your money.

In fact, Lisa's very first home was financed privately by a real estate broker who took a chance on her back in the late 1970s. Lisa put $1,000 down, and the broker financed the rest of that property, which Lisa paid back over time. That was a private loan. It wasn't even a seller-financed loan, because the seller of that home had nothing to do with it. Of course, the broker made interest on that loan, which is why he did it in the first place.

Business brokers could be a good source to find borrowers who need money. You can go online and look up the National Business Brokers Association (NBBA) to find resources in your backyard.

Making Seller-Financed Loans for Mortgages

Private mortgage investors have also branched out into other areas of real estate financing. Here's an example: Alice wants to buy a house in Iowa. The purchase price is $200,000. Alice has $50,000 in cash, and she can get a bank loan for $100,000, but she still needs a $50,000 second mortgage. Now suppose Cheryl, the seller, needs to move. She's downsizing out of the house in which she raised her children, and she wants to buy a small condo for her retirement. If the property is free and clear, Cheryl could say to Alice, "Okay, I'm willing to take a $50,000 second mortgage on the house: a standard 30-year mortgage at a 6 percent interest rate."

But Cheryl would really rather have the cash. She agreed to take the second mortgage only so she could sell her property and move into the condo she wants. In this case, Cheryl can sell those payments to an investor, and that investor can buy those payments and give the cash to Cheryl. Then Alice would be making her payments to that investor (who could be *you*). The second mortgage is a private lending loan that is secured by a piece of real estate. And in today's market, that investor could probably get anywhere from 7 to 10 percent interest on the second mortgage because that's what the market will bear at the time this book is being written.

Obviously, with the recent subprime mortgage disasters and the demise of the real estate industry, the state of the economy today is such that it's going to be a very long time before we see a rebound in the conventional mortgage arena. Therefore, private loans are going to become more and more prevalent. This is why we feel that private lending is such an important topic in this book. It is a type of investing that's beyond the stock market. It is truly investing in alternative ways. We feel savvy investors like you can utilize your money and diversify your portfolio by making private secured loans or purchasing a seller-financed note at a discount. The return to you (that is, your yield) is relatively high and can even exceed 12 percent (depending on how the note was written and the face value of interest on the original documentation), and the investments are ones that you can control.

If Alice, the homeowner, doesn't pay that second mortgage, the investor can come in and foreclose on Alice and take that property back. The investor is in a pretty good position to do that. So the security for that loan is the house. We do want to caution that buying seller-financed mortgages that are secured by real estate is risky today as values of real estate continue to depreciate in many places. The key to avoiding that type of loss is to buy the right mortgages in the first place.

We personally receive between 15 and 20 calls and e-mails *every week* from people asking if we're interested in buying these types of mortgages, and we're doing absolutely nothing to advertise or promote that we're interested in making these types of loans. One reason we get so many of these calls is, of course, because of Lisa's most recent book, *Wise Women Invest in Real Estate*, and her blog, www.wisewomeninvestor.com, where she discusses investing and current issues that pertain to the investor. She also knows people and private mortgage brokers from whom she has bought seller-financed mortgages in the past.

Here's how seller-financed mortgages work. After Cheryl takes on Alice's second mortgage and Alice starts making her payments to Cheryl, Cheryl can assign that mortgage for cash to someone else. An investor in second mortgages (for example, Lisa) could buy that second note. The investor receives payments for the rest of the term that the note was structured for, until it's paid. However, in Lisa's case, she isn't going to pay $50,000 to Cheryl for that second mortgage. Why not? Because of the time value of money. Money 30 years from now is going to be worth a lot less than money today. So Lisa is going to want a significant discount to buy that loan.

At that point, Lisa and Cheryl start negotiating. Why does Cheryl, the seller, want to sell that second mortgage? One reason is that Cheryl wants to be out of this property emotionally—she just wants to move on in her life. She wants to be in her condo, and she wants cash now rather than an income stream over the next 30 years. So what's that worth to Cheryl? It certainly isn't worth $50,000 to Lisa. So Lisa and Cheryl would have a conversation about the value of that property: what it's really worth, and how's the local economy there in that town in Iowa. And if Alice doesn't pay, what recourse does Lisa have? Obviously, Lisa can foreclose on Alice, but how quickly could Lisa sell that property in a fire sale if she had to? Plus, a second mortgage is not as valuable as a first mortgage, because the first mortgage is in the first position in the case of default. This makes the loan riskier for Lisa, so the discount would be deeper for this reason as well. Based on the information that Lisa gets from Cheryl, Lisa would come up with a price.

According to *Noteworthy* magazine, the nationwide average discount on a seller-financed first mortgage is about

20 percent; on a second mortgage, the discount is even higher. And because so many institutional banks that formerly bought seller-financed mortgages are no longer buying them, the discounts have increased. So the discount on this second mortgage could be as high as 50 percent. In other words, Lisa might pay only $25,000 to buy this $50,000 note. Now does that seem fair to Cheryl, the seller? Well, it's what the market will bear. It's up to the seller to make that decision. If the seller really wants to be out of that deal, and Lisa's willing to pay $25,000 for the right to receive these payments over 30 years to get $50,000 plus interest back, it's a good deal for Cheryl. As the economy continues to deteriorate, the need for sellers to divest of this income stream for cash that can be used today will become more and more prevalent.

Here's what's happening in the seller-financed mortgage arena: In many areas in the United States, most notably Florida, California, Arizona, and Las Vegas (which is the worst in the country right now), the property values have gone down. So every week, the appraisal on a particular property could change. The discount will vary depending on where you, as a private investor, want to invest in seller-financed mortgages. The worse the market and the lower the appraisal, the more of a discount your seller will be willing to take to get cash today.

One way to protect yourself when buying a seller-financed mortgage at a discount is to buy a *partial interest* in the seller-financed mortgage. In this case, you would say to the seller something like this: "Because the economy is currently trending downward and property values are continually declining instead of going up, and based on your local real estate market, you [the seller] might be better off allowing us [the investors] to buy a partial interest in your property. So why don't we buy the first five years of payments for $10,000, and then we could buy the next five years of payments for another $10,000, and so forth, until the $50,000 is exhausted."

This way, sellers don't feel like they're going to be taking such a significant discount on the mortgage. You, on the other hand, are still buying those payments in partial increments. You're placing your private money for only $10,000 for those five years of payments (or whatever you negotiate for those five years of payments), and you're making a decent return on your money. Buying a partial interest in a mortgage is a good way for a private investor to buy into seller-financed mortgages, especially if you have an option to buy the next installment.

Finally, there are still areas in the United States where real estate is going up in value—for example, in Wenachi, Washington, where properties are expected to go up an additional 10 percent in the next year (at the time of this writing). Wenachi is a cute little town about three hours from Seattle, up in the hills, with only about 35,000 people, and it has been rated as one of the top places for people looking to relocate in retirement. Because Washington has no state income tax, it's a good market to invest in. If we were presented with a seller-financed mortgage in that particular area that met our requirements—that is, the loan-to-value ratio was sound, there was equity in the deal, and we felt comfortable with the investment—we would make that deal. The point here is that you need to look at each seller-financed mortgage on its own merits. (Note: The *loan-to-value ratio* is the loan amount divided by the current fair market value of the real estate.)

Making Private Loans Based on Commercial Real Estate

Let's look at a different way to make loans to real estate developers. We know an entrepreneur named Barbara who builds government clinics with the help of investors who lend her the money to build. She doesn't secure those loans because she needs the cash infusion. The government isn't involved in any of the lending agreements; it simply signs a long-term lease with Barbara. So Barbara needs to acquire cash that's unsecured to be able to build the clinic, and she's willing to pay a better-than-market-rate return on the interest to any investors.

Is the investor going to get paid back? In this specific case, yes, because Barbara has made many of these deals, and her track record shows that investors do get paid. She realizes the value of investment money and that she could never be successful in building government hospitals if she didn't have the help of these investors who have loaned her the money in the first place. She protects her investors by putting three to six months of monthly payments in a third-party escrow account via an attorney. If she were to default, her investors could go into that escrow account and get those funds.

Is it roll-of-the-dice money? It depends. If you decide to lend anyone money for anything—whether secured or unsecured—it is vital that you do the necessary due diligence to make sure you know what you are lending and how you will get paid and when. Do any of us ever really know what's going to happen to a person's ability to pay? Another way to put this, did any of us know what was going to happen to the money we invested in the stock market? Did we know if the market was going up or down? Did anyone expect the market to plunge the way it did in late 2008 and to continue to be volatile? An unsecured loan is like anything else in life: you take the risk, knowing it is truly unsecured.

The documentation and the due diligence for an unsecured loan is simply a note that says something like "I promise to pay $100,000 over 12 months at 12½ percent interest unsecured." With a note secured by real estate, you have a promise to pay as well, but the security is the real estate on 123 Main Street, and if you don't get paid, the mortgage instrument acts as security with which you can foreclose on that loan.

The main difference in the types of private lending arrangements is whether the loan is secured or not. That is an important distinction. If you're nervous about making private loans or seller-financed mortgages, you should look at only secured loans. If you feel comfortable with the person you're lending money to—maybe it's a family member or a relative, or it's a friend who's been in business for a long time, and you understand what that person is trying to do with the money—it's your call and it's your decision whether to make an unsecured loan. In this book, we're not saying that unsecured loans are either good or bad or that secured loans are either good or bad. We have made both types of loans, and we feel very comfortable making both types of loans. Furthermore, you can secure a loan in many different ways: You can use cars, planes, trains, automobiles, and really any type of personal property for collateral.

Making Private Loans Based on Land Development

Here's another way to make private loans: using land as collateral. A lot of private lenders like to invest in land deals. Land banking can involve someone who has acquired a large parcel of land, has already subdivided the land, and wants to sell the subdivided lots but can't. Or it can involve investor land bankers issuing a grant deed to the investor for the acquired land.

The risk is the location. Generally, these tracts of land are in the middle of nowhere. Investors invest in that land themselves, or they can arrange a private placement with the land developing company. The investors don't get the deed, and the developing company is responsible for making the payments to the investor. In other words, the land developer pays the investors back directly. Many investors like land development deals because they believe land will always have value. Their philosophy is that there is only so much land, so eventually there will be no more land for sale—especially land that has water on it.

In certain parts of the United States, such as Nevada and even some parts of California, people are still purchasing and investing in land. These investors work through land bankers or land brokers. If you're interested in learning more about land banking, you can easily find land bankers and brokers on the Internet. Many conduct land banking seminars that are open to private investors who invest via both their IRAs and their personal funds for low-dollar loans. For example, we recently saw one presentation in which the loans started at $17,000, and these were secured by land.

Judy is a friend in Montana who purchased a $275,000 parcel of land in Missoula, Montana. The land was in foreclosure. Judy decided to buy this land and get it rezoned into commercial building lots. She now has 48 building lots that she can sell. To develop the infrastructure for these building lots, she needs water, septic, and sewer systems. So she needs more cash. She paid the $275,000 in cash to buy the land parcel, and now she needs *more* cash to put in the infrastructure.

So she has come to a circle of friends, a small women's investment group that she runs in Montana, to ask them if they would like to be partners with her in this project. Judy is willing to put this project up as collateral for the money she needs to be able to develop these lots. Her plan, which she has shared with this women's investment group, is to take the 48 lots and offer them on a lottery system to developers or rich investors. The land parcel is located in an area where wealthy second-home buyers (like Ted Turner) own ranches. She estimates that these lots will sell for more than $100,000 a piece.

Does Judy have a good plan? Is the investor secured? These are the questions that, as a private investor, you need to ask yourself every single time you are presented with an opportunity. If we personally lived in this area, we would invest in this project because Judy's been a land developer for 25 years, so she knows her market, and $275,000 on this big parcel is a steal. The amount of money that she needs to raise to install the infrastructure is almost the same amount of money that she paid for the land initially. It's a 50 percent loan-to-value ratio overall, divided by the number of investors. She has made it very affordable for people to buy individual lots with low down payments or very low loans. So if she needed, say, $500,000, she would need only 10 investors with $50,000 each, and the investments would be secured by the building lots in the parcel, which will be selling for more than $100,000 each.

We can't tell you how this deal turned out because it's still in the works. But we can tell you that if we lived in that area, this deal would be a no-brainer for us because it's a very safe, secure loan. Judy is going to develop this land,

and she's got a specific timeline. In a year and a half, she should be able to have all the infrastructure in place, and she should have the roads paved up to the project. Then she's going to sell these 48 lots at $100,000 a piece—which means, of course, that if she sells all of them, she's bringing in $4.8 million. Clearly, she's going to make a lot of money, and anyone who invests with her is going to make a great return on his or her investment. So that would be a great loan—a nice, safe, secured loan. That doesn't mean *you*, our readers, should make transactions like this; you need to decide for yourself whether the terms of this arrangement work for you and whether this type of development project is right for your investing goals. But this is a great illustration of how private lending works.

Our basic philosophy for any type of investing is to look for "the acres of diamonds in your own backyard," which is based on the book *Acres of Diamonds* by Russell H. Conwell, first published in 1915. What this means is that you should invest in what you know, and typically what you know best is local to you (that is, in your own backyard), and if you stick to what's local, you might find "acres of diamonds." So, especially if you're uncomfortable with private lending, you should start small, which means that you should probably start in your own local area. To do that, consider joining local real estate investing clubs and also talking to different mortgage brokers to find out if they ever need any private lending or if they know people who have seller-financed mortgages and need cash.

Here's another example of a private lending deal in Houston, Texas, involving someone we'll call Bill who is in the business of buying small, condemned commercial properties from city government. Bill fixes the properties up, and then he either rents them out on a rent-to-own basis or sells them outright. He looks for one-year financing, but the money he needs to buy and fix up these condemned properties is substantial.

So Bill looks for financing in the Houston area from investors who are not looking to invest their own personal funds, but rather want to invest funds owned by their IRAs. If investors are interested, they lend money as part of a pool. Bill has a local attorney draw up the necessary papers to facilitate this lending pool. The investor who decides to lend money via this pool gets 10 percent interest every single month. The size of the loans range anywhere from $100,000 to $250,000. Bill takes only 6 to 10 people in each pool, and they establish a limited liability corporation (LLC). Then the person who is acquiring the real estate—in this case, Bill—does all the work of buying the condemned property, fixing it up, and finding renters or buyers for the newly renovated property. Bill then pays back the investors in the LLC in one year's time, and he gives them a small percentage of the profit that he made when he sold the building. Investors can find similar good, safe deals in many local areas.

Here's another example. Rich is an attorney in San Diego, California. Five years ago, he got into the business of syndication, which basically means putting together people with fractionalized interest in pools of money and using that money for lending purposes. (In other words, he does what Bill does in Houston but for different types of deals.) Rich is working with a nursing home company in the Midwest to buy a hospital that the nursing home company wants to convert into an assisted-living facility or some other type of health-care facility. Rich is developing a pool of individual investors to lend money into this partnership. The partnership will then buy the building, do all the necessary infrastructure work, and actually stay in the deal with a property management company and a hospital management company to run the health-care facility in the long term.

So if you, as an investor, see a future in assisted-living facilities (and most people probably do because baby boomers are going to need such facilities as they get older), Rich's plan is one that you can invest in today, tomorrow, and well into the future.

Moreover, if you choose to, you can invest in only pieces of the deal. For example, if you want to invest in the syndication for only the limited purpose of acquiring the real estate, you can do that. If you want to stay in the deal so that the company can actually finish the build-out of that real estate and make it into assisted-living facilities, you can do that too. If you want to stay in for the long term, for the renting out of the assisted-living apartments, you can invest in that part of the deal. With private lending, there's a gamut of investing opportunities and time frames. You will run into so many individuals involved in so many different projects and so many different opportunities that finding deals won't be the problem. If you've got cash to lend, it's almost like the green light is on: People who need money will find *you*. So if you're considering private lending as a part of your investing portfolio, know that you're not going to have a problem finding deals. Let's take a look at that in more detail.

How to Find Private Lending Opportunities

If you're going to be lending only within your own community, the best way to find potential investing opportunities is to be very well networked in your community. If you're interested in making loans secured by real estate, contact your local chamber of commerce to find local real estate attorneys, mortgage brokerage associations, and land developers and builders. All of these people and groups will know of individuals who are in a cash-flow situation in which they are looking for private loans from investors like you.

Once you find these organizations, associations, clubs, or other groups, go to one of their meetings. For example, you could go to a meeting of a local Real Estate Investor Association (REIA) or a mortgage association through which private investors lend people money. Let them know you're a private investor and that you'd like to learn about their programs and projects and get involved in using some of your funds to lend money.

Also, work with those individuals who are actively already making private loans, so you can learn how to do it yourself. If you're working through an investing group, if and when the group needs money, they will come to you. You then lend the group the money so that the group can lend money to private individuals.

You can also lend money directly to people, without going through this type of group. For example, you could contact local real estate brokers who can put you in touch with local mortgage brokers who have people who need a loan to facilitate a transaction to either sell their house or buy one.

It is not difficult to develop contacts. The most complicated thing you're going to need to worry about is the paperwork and making sure that the property appraises for what it needs to appraise for. Find a great attorney who knows the real estate business that you're interested in because your attorney will make sure you've crossed all the T's and dotted all the I's in your loan contract. Your attorney will also make sure that your loan is secured by real estate that has title insurance.

There is a wide range of places where you can go to find land deals. Throughout the United States, there are real estate investor associations and hard-money and mortgage associations that deal with private lending. All you need to do is join a local association. The association lends out its own money to individuals, and then the association looks to individual private lenders (investors) like us (the authors) to participate and pay us a return on our money. Here's an example that illustrates how this works.

We recently received solicitations from a company called UniTrust Mortgage and from a company called Dellovo Capital, which claims that it's been in business since 1986 and specializes in the placement of commercial real estate and business financing. We know nothing about either of these companies; they simply mailed us their solicitations, which are essentially marketing pieces. For example, one said, "UniTrust Mortgage has millions of dollars of private investor funds to place, in addition to its institutional loans." The company is contacting private investors, like us, with this pitch: "If you'll lend us $100,000, we'll put that money in a pool. We'll then lend this pool of money (including your investment) out to commercial properties, to apartment buildings, and to multiunit deals of five properties or more. We're going to do only larger deals with your money. We'll pay you 8½ percent a year on your money, and you have to do absolutely nothing. And you're secured by our company, so you can feel comfortable investing your money with us."

If you decide you want to find these types of companies, all you have to do is basically let your fingers do the walking through the Internet or join a local mortgage association. Anybody in the public can join a local mortgage association. But please do your homework first before you jump in, and make sure that the company is for real!

There are companies out there doing this right now, whether it's apartments, offices, retail stores, multifamily housing, mixed-use buildings, industrial and manufacturing facilities, resorts, land, or assisted-living or other medical facilities (health-care real estate is the new hot trend). In addition, there are companies using private investments to finance restaurants, hardware stores, churches, funeral homes, automobile dealers, franchises, gas stations—you name it. You will also find companies that are de novo capital companies or start-up banks: They handle only private placement and private lending to individuals or businesses that want your money. They'll put you in a pool, and you'll have nothing to do with the paperwork or with the decision on where the money is going—in short, you do none of the work.

We are not recommending any of these companies in particular. We're simply telling you that they're out there and easy to find. If you want to place money with companies that make private loans on a large basis, and if you want to use a percentage of your investing portfolio for private lending in these types of companies, you can easily find them on the Internet. Or you can join a local private mortgage association. You should understand that in these situations you're going to be earning a return on your investment of 7 or 8 percent, or maybe 9 percent if you're lucky, and that the company through which you're investing will be earning 12 to 14 percent. That company makes the spread, but if you don't want to do the paperwork yourself for this type of private loan, or if you're worried about getting ripped off or burned, this is a good way to go. You'll earn less interest, but you'll have less work to do, and you might sleep better at night.

You're going to see more and more private lending opportunities emerge as the economy worsens, as credit markets plunge, and as credit card companies start getting into trouble because people aren't going to be able to afford to make their credit card payments. The only way some people are going to be able to get money to fund anything is through private means. Private funding via both individual investors and small investing companies has already increased substantially in the last year. However, as we were writing this book, the future of owner financing and private lending can change with the proposed bill HR 1728, which has been approved by the House of Representatives but has not yet come before the Senate. The bill specifically deals with predatory lending, but it includes a clause relating to seller financing and private lending. Because the bill has not yet been passed, it isn't clear how it will affect the average investor.

Individual borrowers can use lending clubs for various things. Here are two that have been in business for a long time to start your research and understand what they are about:

- www.lendingclub.com
- www.prosper.com

These organizations lend money to individuals and small businesses. They often post their requirements for borrowers (in terms of credit scores and so on) on their Web sites. You can go through these organizations if you want to lend money to qualified loan applicants. Usually, the minimum investment for these types of companies is $5,000, but the amount varies depending on the company's pool and what the company is setting out to do. Again, you can either do the work yourself and make private loans directly to individuals or businesses, or you can lend your money through a third party.

Private lending companies have been around a long, long time. They offer alternative investments for investors wanting to obtain greater returns than they would get from the stock market, CDs, or mutual funds. In most cases, they deal in real estate. They like rehabs, foreclosures, and other distressed properties. They like the fix-up market because they understand it. But there are also companies out there that don't necessarily work only in the real estate arena.

DOING DUE DILIGENCE SO YOU DON'T GET BURNED

When deciding whether a particular loan makes sense to you, here are the facts that you really need to know. First, what is the loan-to-value (LTV) ratio? In other words, if you're using real estate as collateral for your loan, what is the equity in the property? Simply divide the amount of the loan you're considering making by the fair market value of the property.

The next thing you need to know—and it is even more important than the LTV ratio—is the investment-to-value ratio. What is the ratio of the amount of cash you are putting up for the investment to its value today? To see how this works, let's go back to the example of Alice, Cheryl, and Lisa concerning the seller-financed property in Iowa. If Cheryl is putting up $50,000 for the second mortgage so that Alice can buy the property from her, Cheryl needs to make sure that the investment-to-value ratio is below 70 percent. Otherwise, she could get burned by not having enough equity if Alice doesn't pay her back. Before you even consider negotiating on a seller-financed mortgage, you need to know those two factors.

Obviously, you should also know the payment history of the person who wants to borrow money, as well as your borrower's credit score, if you can get it. Note that you cannot get a credit score unless the borrower signs an authorization allowing you to obtain the credit report and score. Hopefully, the seller of the property, who is trying to sell the note, has a credit score for the borrower.

The borrower's credit score and credit history are certainly critical factors because if the borrower can't make payments to you, you obviously don't want to buy a second mortgage, a first mortgage, or any mortgage. You absolutely need to do due diligence, and sometimes that can be a lot of work. That's the major difference between investing with a third party in a traditional investment such as a corporate bond and investing on your own. If you invest on your own in any type of investment, don't you do more work than you would if you were going through a third party? But when you are investing on your own, the risk is the reward, and your return is going to be greater. Utilizing private lending and seller-financed mortgages is an opportunity for you to grow your net worth. Plus, you are betting on your own wealth accumulation directly, rather than allowing someone else to control your money!

Here are some other things to keep in mind when you're doing your due diligence. You should perform a background check on the borrower. You really want to make sure that the borrower has the character to pay back your loan. You want to verify your borrower's income capacity to make sure that he or she can make the monthly payment to you. Make sure your borrower has a decent credit history and has made payments on time. That's very, very important.

You want to make sure that the terms of any private lending agreement are in writing and that the agreement is signed by both parties. The agreement, or promissory note, should clearly state all of the following terms:

- Interest rate on the loan
- Amount to be repaid
- Time period of the loan
- Type of collateral
- Default terms

If the collateral on the loan you're making is real estate, you need a mortgage security interest document. If the collateral on the loan is a business, you need a UCC-1 filing for that business.

Regarding interest, you must charge a minimum interest rate if you're lending money. You cannot make a zero interest loan. The IRS considers a zero interest loan to be a gift, and it will tax you on that gift. As of March 2008, the federal government has set the minimum interest rate to be 4.3 percent.

If you're doing a seller-financed mortgage, enlist the aid of an attorney or an escrow officer to handle the paperwork. We can't emphasize that enough. If you're just getting started as a private lender, regardless of the amount that you are lending and for what, use an attorney, because you don't know what type of paperwork you should have. Fortunately, your attorney will know. After you have some experience—and success—making a few private loans, and you are familiar with the paperwork required, you could make these loans on your own. But in the beginning, we strongly recommend that you hire an attorney to write your loan agreements. Moreover, the laws that pertain to private lending change frequently, so don't assume that you can do this on your own. Hire an attorney!

Handling the Accounting and Getting Paid

Now that you know more about the types of loans that you can make as an investor and how to find opportunities for this type of investment, and once you've done the necessary due diligence to lower your risk and you've hired your attorney to draw up the loan agreements and documents, of course you need to know how to get paid!

Many investors like to have a third party service their notes or loans rather than doing it themselves. What this means is that you hire a note servicing company. So, instead of your borrower making payments directly to you (whether you're lending or buying seller-financed mortgages), your borrower makes payments to a title company or an escrow company.

That company records the payments and then sends you a check (minus a servicing fee, of course). This way, you don't have to handle any of the accounting or the tracking of payments, and you don't have to follow up with your borrower to obtain the payments. It's very simple to find such companies. You can call local title companies to see if they service loans for other people or if they can recommend an escrow company that does.

On the other hand, we take our payments directly, and we do our own accounting. We have a note servicing software program that handles that for us.

Lender Beware: How Not to Get Stiffed

One final point we want to make if you're considering making loans that are not secured by any collateral at all: You need to realize that your chances of getting repaid can be iffy. You really need to know the person you're making that loan to—and even then, you might not get repaid.

We had this happen to us once. Years ago, we made a loan to one of our employees who had run into some financial difficulty. Her husband had lost his job, and they were about to lose their house because they had fallen behind on their mortgage payments. They were three months in arrears. They were getting further and further behind even though she was still working. She didn't know what she was going to do. They had no one to turn to for help; they had nowhere to go. She said her husband was interviewing for jobs, and he hoped to have something within a month. But until he found something, they were naturally very anxious and worried. Because we liked her and felt sorry for her, we loaned her $10,000. The loan was unsecured because she and her husband had nothing to secure it with.

We lent her $10,000 at 10 percent interest, so she would pay back $132.15 a month for 10 years. She made the $132.15 payments for the first six months, but then she stopped paying us. She simply didn't have the money to pay us back because her financial situation was getting worse. We really had no recourse because the loan wasn't secured by any collateral at all. So it's important for you to understand that when you're making unsecured loans, if they are truly unsecured, you take the chance of not getting paid back.

And in this situation, we almost didn't get paid back. In fact, the only reason we did get paid back was because this employee inherited some money when a relative passed away. But if that hadn't happened, we would have lost the money we loaned to our employee. That person still works for us, but we'll never do that again.

Since that loan, we have a policy. We don't make loans to employees or to anyone we work with. We don't even make loans to family. If we're asked to make a loan to someone we know, we look at it as a gift that we don't count on getting back. You don't really want to risk your relationship with your parents, siblings, children, friends, coworkers, or staff. If you want to lend them money, consider it a gift. If they repay you, great. If they don't, forget about it.

Another thing we'd like to caution you about is the late-night TV educational programs and the get-rich-quick schemes that you see on the Internet, both of which advertise how easy it is to get into the loan business or into the note business. If you've seen or heard something that promises that "you too can make millions of dollars doing these deals," you need to be very careful. Buyer beware. Check out the local Better Business Bureau, contact other organizations, contact your state's department of professional regulation and licensing, and make sure the people offering these deals are legitimate, because there are thousands of people who have made millions of dollars off innocent individuals who think they're lending money for a variety of different cash flows and have gotten burned. Again, *buyer beware*, and *do your due diligence before you lend any money*.

Finally, again, *don't do anything without a good attorney*, one who understands the business you're investing in. If you're going to enter into real estate transactions, hire a real estate attorney. If you're going to lend money to businesses, hire a business attorney. It is definitely worth your investment of a few hundred bucks to get at least one correct document prepared that you can reuse over and over again.

In this chapter, we've covered private lending extensively for an important reason: We believe that private lending is fast becoming the norm. Just try to go out and refinance your personal residence. Thirty-year mortgage rates are at 4.5 percent as we write this book, but just try to get the bank to refinance your property. And if it does, the fees associated with the new loan are outrageous! So the only way that people might be able to borrow money is through other people.

CHAPTER 3

INVESTING IN PRECIOUS METALS

Gold, Silver, Platinum, Palladium, and Titanium

When most people hear the words "investing in precious metals," what comes to mind is investing in gold and silver—actual *physical* gold and silver, either in coins or bullion. But there are other ways to invest in gold and silver—specifically, in the form of gold certificates and silver certificates. You might also be interested in investing in other precious metals, such as platinum, palladium, and titanium.

This chapter covers all these topics and provides valuable information (no pun intended) on what to expect when you buy precious metals as well as information about the true, long-term value of what you've bought. The chapter also covers how not to get scammed and how to protect your investment by doing the necessary due diligence before you buy. Throughout the chapter, we share stories of our own investments as well as examples from other precious metals investors.

Why People Buy Gold: A Hedge against Inflation

Before we get into the nitty-gritty of how to invest in precious metals, we want to clarify right up front that there's a distinction between *buying* a precious metal such as gold or silver as a currency and *investing* in gold or silver. If you want to *invest* in precious metals, you need to buy and own stock in a company that does that. Personally, we've never done that. And the reason we haven't is that we believe the whole purpose of buying coins is to own the actual coins.

Most people buy gold as a hedge against currency running wild and against inflationary pressures. As long as you have gold, it always retains its *intrinsic* value. So people will always be willing to exchange goods or services for gold because gold is *real* money. Money is categorized in two types: fiat currency and specie. Fiat currency is the paper money that is issued by governments; therefore, it is a substitute currency. It is the dollar bill we carry around or any other form of paper money in any country. In contrast, specie is actual hard money that has intrinsic value. That's the difference between the two types of currency: one is real, and the other is a substitute for something that has real value.

That's why most people buy gold as a currency. If fiat currency decreases in value, gold still retains its intrinsic value. Gold isn't affected by inflation, which is why many people like to own gold. It retains its purchasing power regardless of what has happened to prices because of inflation. Our friend James Turk, who is a gold investor and the founder of GoldMoney (www.goldmoney.com), has a nice explanation for how the value of gold remains stable. If your grandfather bought a Saville Row suit 100 years ago with gold coins, it would cost you the same amount of gold coins that your grandfather used 100 years ago to buy the same suit on Saville Row today, for the same price. That's the utility of gold as a currency.

When people buy gold, what they do is exchange their fiat currency that they have today for bars of gold. Of course, you have to find a place to store your gold. For example, James owns gold bars, which he keeps in a London bank vault. He actually has a separate vault just for his gold. In fact, James has a business through which he buys and sells gold bars, and we have placed some of our money into this business.

Note that we didn't say we "invested" our money in gold via James; instead, we "placed" our money in gold via James. Again, this is the distinction we're making—that gold is not an investment because it doesn't appreciate—or increase—in value, so you're not going to make 10 or 20 percent on your money when you use it to buy gold. Therefore, you should buy gold only if you're interested in *not losing money* because gold simply *retains* its value over time.

Since James has a business of buying and selling gold, he's obviously not the average investor, so let's look at how the average investor (for example, you) could buy gold. Suppose you want to buy five bars of gold. One way to do this is to contact the Delaware Depository Service Company (DDSC) and buy either coins of various denominations or gold bars from them. (Full disclosure: We have a business relationship with the DDSC.) Buying gold coins is not a bad idea if you are going to use the gold as currency because the gold is already denominated. In other words, if you know what the weight of the gold coin is and what the value of it is, it's very easy to carry around and store.

In contrast, the smallest gold bars you can buy are 40 ounces, which makes them tough to carry around because they're so heavy. A 40-ounce gold bar is about 4 inches by 1½ inches by ¼ of an inch, similar in size to a Hershey chocolate bar. So if you decide you want to buy gold bars and have them delivered to you, you could put them in a shoebox at the bottom of the closet—which is what a friend recently told us she does, believe it or not. In fact, many people keep money in various forms in their homes—whether in gold bars, gold coins, or cash. This is typically called "mattress money."

There's a substantial risk, of course, to keeping money in your home. If that money is stolen, or if your house burns down or is destroyed in a hurricane or tidal wave or earthquake, that mattress money is gone forever. There's no way to protect mattress money or to insure it. But if you deposit your money into a bank account, there's insurance for it. If you don't trust the government's FDIC protection or the bank itself, you can convert your mattress money into specie, like gold or silver, and put it in a safe vault, somewhere that you are confident will be safe in the event of insurrection, revolution, or natural disaster.

How We Got Started in Gold: Buying Coins from the Government

Hugh started seriously investing in precious metals in 1981, and he has continued to buy gold coins since then. The process hasn't changed a lot since 1981. Buying gold coins is actually a tradition in Hugh's family. It's a fairly strong tradition among Europeans, as well as among Americans who lived during the Depression. Hugh looked at this not as collecting coins, which is entirely different (we describe this in more detail at the end of this chapter), but as a hedge against fiat currency inflation. As we mentioned earlier, fiat currency can end up having no value, whereas gold and silver have always had some kind of intrinsic value.

Hugh was living in Austria at the time, and he started buying gold coins from the Austrian government by way of Austrian banks, which sell old coins from the Austrian government to the general public. There's quite a business in doing that because people know that they are buying government coins directly from a bank. They know their purchase is safe because the government does not have a reputation of ripping people off and giving them phony coins. (Similarly, years ago, the U.S. government mandated that people could make investments in IRAs, for example, only in U.S. government–minted gold eagles and silver eagles, but there's more to that story.) As mentioned, buying gold is a family tradition for many people, as it was in Hugh's family. His grandfather bought coins, and Hugh's mother used to give him gold coins regularly, always on the basis of this scarcity mentality: "If you ever need it, here are some gold coins." It was simply something his family did, so Hugh also started putting money into gold coins in 1981.

And it was and is very simple to buy them. You simply walk into a bank and say, "I would like to buy gold coins." And the teller asks, "How many would you like?" Then the teller quotes the price for the coin because there is usually a charge involved in buying coins. You can buy single gold or silver coins or rolls of coins. Hugh has bought coins from time to time on no set schedule and not according to any plan or price point. And because he has bought the gold coins as a hedge against inflation, he has not sold a single one of them.

Buying Silver Coins from Dealers

In the 1990s, Hugh got more serious about buying coins. At one time, it was possible to buy bags of silver coins in the United States because silver coins were still in circulation until 1964 (when the U.S. mints increased the amount of copper in coins). Hugh started buying silver coins when they were at their lowest prices and selling them for slightly higher prices. Many people at that time were buying and selling silver, especially silver dollars (and some gold coins, but in the 1970s and 1980s, there weren't a lot of gold coins in circulation).

Hugh bought silver dollars in bags of thousands, typically 10 bags at a time, which were being traded (that is, bought and sold) by coin dealers in the United States rather than by banks, as they were in Austria. This was a way that people could buy silver easily without having to deal with silver bars, and they could then subdivide the bags of coins if they wanted to. The only downside to buying coins this way was that the bags were very heavy—in fact, Hugh used a portable trolley to carry the bags of coins out to his car.

Hugh found coin dealers simply by looking in the Yellow Pages. Today, you would more likely search on the Internet. The nice thing about buying a bag of silver dollars was that you could look at the silver dollars and see whether or not they were real silver. It's difficult to manufacture a phony silver dollar, and it's not cost effective anyway, so buying silver coins was very safe. Buyers were well assured that the silver dollars they bought were real. People could then sell their bags of silver dollars, primarily to other dealers, and they made money on the spread. In other words, they bought the coins at a low price, and then they sold them at a higher price.

Hugh got to know several coin dealers with whom he shopped regularly, and he could see the difference in their pricing. Hugh made as much as 10 percent in a couple of weeks just by buying from one dealer and selling to another. Silver prices were, and still are, very volatile. Hugh also bought from private individuals who had coins that they wanted to get rid of because they needed the money. It's easy to find such people just by hanging around coin dealerships and coin shops. You get to know who the reputable dealers are, then you start to see other individuals around there too, and you hang out with these people. People who deal in gold and silver and coin get to know one another. It was really a free market, and it still is to an extent.

The most Hugh ever paid for a bag was $6 per coin, which was $6,000 for a bag, which he then sold for $7,000 only two weeks later. Again, silver is very, very volatile. Hugh also bought and held silver coins for a fairly long period of time, selling when the price was up.

Hugh eventually stopped buying and selling silver regularly because it became too much work. He decided instead to be a consultant and get into the retirement business, which was a lot more interesting.

BEWARE OF COIN SCAMS

Buying and selling coins was a really good business for many people, so a few coin dealers decided to form limited partnerships so that they could accumulate large amounts of other people's money and tell those people that they were investing in coins. Then they would buy and sell the paper that represented the coins that they were allegedly buying. Unfortunately, they weren't really buying any coins; they were just scamming their investors—which is another reason we advocate that if you're interested in buying gold and silver, you should buy *actual* gold and silver coins or bars. After all, what's the point in being in specie if somebody merely gives you a piece of paper or some kind of fiat note that *says* you own specie but you don't really *have* the specie? (Of course, that's the basis of gold certificates, which Lisa has invested in. We'll tell you more about that later in this chapter, because there are gold certificates and there are gold certificates.)

Anyway, one of the most notorious of these limited partnerships was called California Coin. Many people who invested in this company lost a lot of money. Although the smallest investment you could make was $10,000, there were some who invested—and lost—a quarter of a million dollars. The way this one worked is that people invested in the limited partnership rather than the actual metal. The company was supposed to be investing in metal: real dollars, real gold, and other precious metals. But these investments lost money—so much money that there wasn't any left for the investors. Like other con artists, the only people who made any money were the purveyors of the limited partnership. The investors didn't receive certificates that said they owned a certain amount of gold or silver. Instead, they received certificates that said they were members of a limited partnership. So watch out. Don't invest in a business; invest in the actual precious metals.

The investors could not even seek recourse from the original partners of California Coin because the founding partners just declared bankruptcy and said, "Oh, gee, we're sorry." Their defense was, "Nobody said we were giving them [our investors] coin. We just said we were giving them limited partnership interest." They may have been scum, but they weren't the only ones who scammed people this way. There were many others like them, and there will continue to be others like them, who have no trouble taking other people's investments.

Personally, we didn't invest in these types of companies simply because of our philosophy about fiat currency versus specie. If we want to invest in gold coin or silver coin, we go for the real thing. But let's now look at the pros and cons of buying gold or silver certificates.

BUYING CERTIFICATED GOLD

As mentioned, Hugh didn't ever like the idea of having certificated gold or silver, or buying into LLCs, or goldmines, or mining stock. When you buy mining stock, which is traded on stock markets today, you're buying a stock certificate in that *mining company*; you're not buying real gold or real platinum or real silver or any real metal. Instead, you're investing in the operations of the company whose stock you're buying. That type of investing is just like buying into a diamond mine. If you buy shares of De Beers, for example, you don't receive diamonds as a dividend. The difference between the investing strategies is that in one you are speculating on the success of a company that develops gold or silver, and in the other you are holding actual gold or silver in coins or bars.

In other words, one approach is, "I believe this investment is going to go up because these guys at this company are going to do some wonderful things, and they're going to make me a lot of money via their operations." The other approach is, "I want to *place* my money—not *invest* it—into gold and silver that I hold myself because I want it as a hedge in the event that there is runaway inflation"—such as there was, for example, in the Myanmar Republic. Some individuals are in one camp, some in the other, and some in both.

The mistake that many people make is that they believe they're investing if they bought gold when it was $400 an ounce, say, in 1981, and then sold that gold recently when it was at $900. If you think you more than doubled your money by "buying low and selling high," you've forgotten about inflation. After all, what is the value of the dollar that you're selling it at? Again, *gold has never been a good investment* because it only retains its intrinsic value. Remember what our friend James Turk said: You can buy the same quality Saville Row suit in 1900 and in 2000 for the same amount of gold.

But let's move on to gold in certificate form. In stark contrast to the horrible experience of the California Coin LLP investors, in which they found that their certificates weren't in coin at all but merely in the operations of a poorly run company, there are certificated forms of gold that one can trust. For example, we have a relationship with the Perth Mint, which is owned by the government of Western Australia. The Perth Mint is a mining, smelting, and refining operation in Perth, the largest city in Western Australia. The Perth Mint digs gold out of the ground in Australia, refines it, melts it, and then stores it in a huge storage facility that is full of gold bars. If you want to buy gold, instead of shipping it to you or putting your gold bars into your own little vault (which other gold storage facilities do if you want them to), the Perth Mint's approach is to say, "We're going to make it economical for you to own the gold in this vault. We guarantee that the gold is real gold and that it is guaranteed by the government of Western Australia."

Because of that guarantee, we're willing to take the chance that the government of Western Australia is not in league with bad people who are mining theoretical gold, as stock companies might do. The Western Australian government actually guarantees the gold. It audits the gold, examines it, and makes sure that it's real gold in the Perth Mint vaults. Lisa bought a $50,000 Perth Mint certificate. She has a warehouse receipt that is guaranteed by the government of Western Australia to actually have gold for the receipt for which she paid $50,000 at that time.

We went to Perth to check out the operation before Lisa invested. We also wanted to establish a relationship with the Perth Mint so that our Entrust clients could do business with the mint. We had to prove to the mint operators that we were real people and that we weren't flimflammers or con artists. At the same time, we had to prove to ourselves that the mint operators were trustworthy. We toured the mines at Kalgoorlie, which are about 400 miles northeast of Perth and are located in the Eastern Goldfields, named during an 1893 gold rush there. We saw the presentation on how the Perth Mint mines gold, we saw where its warehouse is, we spoke with the executives, and we had a jolly good time learning how they work.

Of course, we weren't allowed to take pictures of the vault because that would compromise the security. Also, the average investor is not given the grand tour. The only reason we were allowed to tour the facility is because we represent 50,000 investors who may be interested in doing business with them, so we were establishing a bank-to-bank relationship. Rest assured, however, that the mint's gold vault is indeed huge, like the U.S. Bullion Depository at Fort Knox, Kentucky, which holds 4,600 tons of gold and is second only to the Federal Reserve Bank's underground vault in New York City, which holds 5,000 metric tons of gold.

Again, for security reasons, the general public can't tour vaults or depositories to see the gold and silver or other valuables that are stored there. The vault or depository hires auditors from firms like PricewaterhouseCoopers to take a physical inventory of what's being stored there, to validate and verify that the gold or silver is really there. In fact, when we went to visit the Perth Mint, the managers let us see only the building; they didn't allow us inside. They simply pointed at it and said, "It's over there." We weren't even allowed to take pictures of the building. If you visit the Perth Mint, you are only allowed entry to a small room, where you are shown pictures of the showroom and the mine. All you really see of the operation is the huge dump trucks that are constantly coming and going from the mine. These trucks have tires that are 2½ times the height of an average person and are about 15 feet across. Just one of these dump trucks delivers only one golf ball–sized gold nugget from all the dirt it carries. These trucks run day and night. If you start doing the math on the number of trucks, multiplied by the number of trips, multiplied by the number of golf ball–sized gold nuggets, you realize there's a lot of gold in that mine. And the gold mine is enormous. It's many miles wide, and the mine operators are obviously digging many tons of dirt.

So, after seeing the operation, we decided it was worth buying $50,000 of gold certificates from the Perth Mint. And our investors at Entrust have also bought gold certificates. As always, if you want to purchase warehouse receipts or certificated forms of precious metals, you must perform due diligence on both the physical bullion and the certificated forms. If you can't go to Perth, or even if you go to Perth but you can't get in to see the vault that houses your gold, you need to find some other way to get the information that you need to make an informed decision before you put your money down.

Buying Coins as Collectibles

Buying coins as collectibles is very different from buying gold or silver coins as a hedge against inflation, which is, in essence, buying coins to use as currency. Coin collectors who buy gold or silver coins actually have more in common with people who collect fine art, antiques, jewels, or rare stamps. Moreover, collecting coins is also not investing. For example, if you found an old gold Greek or Roman or Persian coin, it would have a huge amount of value because of its *collectible* value. The actual *gold* value in that coin is relatively small. The coin's value is that of a rare historical item.

For example, when Hugh visited India, he met people in villages who were hoarders of gold. They searched for and found ancient antiquities that archaeologists would love to get their hands on, just from a historic point of view. But these villagers didn't care one way or another about the historic value. They just cared when something was gold. They melted down the coins and other objects for their *intrinsic* value. Of course, the *historic* value, and the value of these gold coins or gold artifacts as art objects, was much, much higher than the value of the actual gold. And after they melted it down, it's just gold, and no longer has any historic or aesthetic value.

Because they need to eat, many villagers do this all over India and other poor countries. If you're starving, the archaeological and historic point of view is not important to you. Archaeologists view this as destroying the real worth of the object, but to the villagers who find these artifacts, it's not destruction. For them, the real worth is in the gold, which can buy them food.

This is why Europeans and many Americans who lived through the Depression buy gold and silver coins because they know that when they need money to eat or for any other survival reason, they can simply use their gold and silver. We know many people who have silver coins in their collections, like cartwheels (U.S. silver dollars, also known as Morgan dollars) and half dollars and silver quarters and Mercury dimes. Many people who were born during the Depression or who lived during its immediate aftermath held onto these coins. They feel secure in that they can always use these coins for real currency to buy the goods they would need. Even if that's just a loaf of bread.

Investing in Platinum, Palladium, and Titanium

Some people think that investing in platinum, palladium, and titanium is similar to investing in truly precious metals like gold and silver. You *can* buy platinum, palladium, and titanium in bar form (for example, in 10-ounce bars), the way you can buy gold and silver. You can typically buy them from the same people who sell gold and silver bars.

But why would you want to? After all, platinum, palladium, and titanium have never been used as currency, as gold and silver have. They are not a hedge against inflation, as gold is. And you certainly won't find ancient Roman coins made out of these metals. Platinum, palladium, and titanium are really commodities and, as such, investing in them is like investing in any other commodity.

But when you buy these metals, you have the same decision to make that you have when you buy gold or silver: Do you get a certificate or a warehouse receipt that says you own *x* ounces of platinum, or do you take physical delivery? It's up to each investor to decide. We are seeing more investors who want to take physical possession or who want to have their bars stored in a facility that they're comfortable with. But if you elect to take physical possession of the metal you buy, what do you do with it? We have clients who buy platinum bars, some through GoldMoney and some through the Delaware Depository Service Company (both of which we mentioned earlier in the chapter), and some through one of the many other dealers in this business.

Many people don't even know what palladium is, so there isn't much of a market for it. Because only a few people are interested in it, the rest of the world may be wondering "Why would I invest in this?" And if you don't know what it is, you shouldn't be investing in it. In fact, people use palladium every day without even knowing it, because the catalytic converters in all cars have palladium in them. The value of palladium is very volatile. Because it's used primarily in cars, and because the demand for automobiles worldwide has plummeted, there isn't as much need for palladium recently as there used to be. The value of palladium went down 30 percent in 2008.

So, once again, you need to do your due diligence. If you're interested in investing in palladium, you need to know what it's used for and what the current worldwide demand is. Why would you buy palladium bars when it's a fungible commodity that can be used in manufacturing, and you can't convert a bar of palladium into its use in catalytic converters—at least not easily. Also, more than 50 percent of palladium comes from Russia, which is not exactly a stable country. That supply uncertainty also contributes to the volatility of palladium prices, because prices could be driven up by restricting the flow of palladium to bring more cash into Russia. So you need to be a really informed investor to make decisions about investing in palladium.

It is a little easier to consider investing in platinum. Some people think platinum is a currency hedge like gold, but it never has been. One reason is that platinum wasn't really popularized as a jewelry item until the 1950s and 1960s. It's a rather dull metal, and it never caught on like gold and silver, which of course have been around for centuries.

Titanium, like platinum, is used for jewelry, and it's also used in surgery (for example, hip replacements are made of titanium). However, the biggest use of titanium is in the military. It's heavily used in aerospace projects because it's incredibly lightweight and extremely strong. Because its use in the jewelry market is not significant (in the way that the use of silver and gold and even platinum is), titanium is another commodity, and its price fluctuates widely because demand for it fluctuates widely. Like the palladium market, the titanium market is relatively volatile.

We've included platinum, palladium, and titanium in this book because there are people who are interested in them and view them as alternative investments. But these metals are used mostly in industrial products, so we don't consider them alternative investments, like gold and silver.

CHAPTER

INVESTING IN NATURAL RESOURCES

Natural resources, by definition, are naturally occurring, and many of them are also nonrenewable. The demands of the 6.76 billion people living, consuming, and, unfortunately, exhausting the world's natural resources are placing enormous pressure on the ability of our planet to regenerate some of these resources. However, from an investment point of view, the scarcity of natural resources and the demand for them makes them potentially economically viable.

This chapter covers alternative investing opportunities in five natural resources—solar power (which we also cover from a different angle in Chapter 5), water, oil, coal, and natural gas—and it provides examples of people who have invested successfully and those who have been financially burned.

Solar power is the only inexhaustible natural resource. In some ways, solar power has always powered the economics of the planet, even before we arrived. After all, sun makes plants grow. Water is a natural resource that is exhaustible in the form that we like to use it—to grow food, produce electricity (which includes ocean salt water from tidal action), and drink. Petroleum is a natural resource that, in its transmuted form, generates power and heat and plastics. Coal and natural combustible gas are used for similar purposes as petroleum.

INVESTING IN SOLAR POWER

Solar power has been used for thousands of years, but the early uses were mostly passive. The ancient Greeks and Romans were the first people credited with taking advantage of the power of the sun simply by building their homes to face the sun to provide them with light and heat. And, of course, many people still do this today. Fast forward many centuries to 1861, when the first steam engine powered by the sun was invented, but the high cost to run it made it prohibitively expensive to use. Albert Einstein was awarded the 1921 Nobel Prize in Physics for his research on the photoelectric effect, which was key to generating electricity through solar cells. And in 1953, Bell Labs developed the first solar cell capable of generating an electric current.

Still, not much was done with all this research and study until 1973, when the Arab oil embargo finally woke up the world to its dependence on oil and the fact that oil is not limitless and will eventually be fully expended. It was then that scientists, researchers, and governments started to explore alternative sources of power, including solar power. In the decades since then, industry has made huge strides in solar power development, and today, the photovoltaic market is growing at about 30 percent a year.[1]

Because solar power has become economically viable, we see solar power companies springing up everywhere. The more people there are and the less oil there is, the more interest consumers have in solar panels and electric cars. (However, we recently traveled to India, which has more than a billion people, and oddly enough, we found little interest in electric cars. We also saw very few solar panels on rooftops in India. Go figure.)

Solar power is of great interest to consumers today because of the cost of petroleum. Although the price of petroleum has come down from its levels during the summer of 2008, prices are still pretty high, and they will continue to increase over time. They might not rise too much in the very short term, but we look at money and investing from the long view—10 to 20 years from now. We believe that over the next two decades, the world will see the decline of petroleum as a resource and that alternative energy forms like solar power will become even more important. The use of solar power has grown internationally for the past 10 years, with Denmark and Germany leading the way in Europe. In the United States, however, solar power is just really starting to contribute only about 1 percent of our energy needs. In absolute terms, the growth is small, but percentage-wise, solar power development has been expanding.

For investors in solar power, two different markets exist: the large national companies and the small local companies. In terms of the national (and international) companies, several large entities are getting into the business. About a dozen companies produce solar cells, which come in different

---

[1] "A Brief History of Solar Energy," www.southface.org.

kinds of arrays. As the industry continues to expand, a small investor can do relatively well in this particular arena because people are inventing new opportunities in solar energy. Here are a few examples of the larger entities:

- In Sunnyvale, California, SunPower Corporation, a pioneer in the field, produces high-efficiency solar cells that allow the amount of wattage that one can get out of a unit cost to be competitive with a coal-fired plant.
- In China, Suntech Power is looking at reducing manufacturing costs to decrease China's dependence on oil. They're not exporting their materials yet.
- In Japan, Sharp Computing is the leading provider of solar cells. It produces 15 percent of the worldwide solar cell and module supply. Sharp is also heavily involved in the U.S. market.

With these larger companies, investing in them is handled primarily through traditional ways, that is, buying stock via the stock exchange. Of course, buying a company's stock isn't making an alternative investment in the way in which we are focusing in this book. With respect to alternative investing, you need to look at innovative companies, which are smaller companies or local companies that are involved in producing these kinds of energy replacements.

This investing principle applies to any kind of energy replacement technology, whether it's coal or oil or gas. Another investment opportunity is related to clean coal. Actually, clean coal is not exactly clean because the only way to get coal to be "clean" is to cook it and make a gas out of it, which produces a by-product of carbon dioxide that must be disposed. In response, companies that are developing ways of burying CO_2 in the ground or at the bottom of the ocean are springing up, which offers another investment opportunity.

So there are investment opportunities not only in the natural resource itself but also in the by-products created in the use of the resource. This introduces a market that many people have missed. A large industry has emerged to meet the need to process the waste products that result from the production and use of natural resources. There are companies that take the waste products from things that we've produced, and they regenerate them and restore them into some manner that can be reused, or they bury them forever.

INVESTING IN WATER RIGHTS AND WATER TREATMENT PROJECTS

Another alternative investing opportunity that many people aren't aware of is water, because potable water isn't always available everywhere. A few savvy individuals, in the United States in particular, have discovered the ability to purchase water rights. In the United States, a landowner owns the rights to the surface of the property, but not necessarily to what is underneath. Another entity or individual can own the rights to the water and minerals underneath it. Those rights are sold separately from the land rights.

When there is an expanding economy, as occurred in the United States during the twentieth century, there's an enormous demand for water for personal consumption and agriculture. That water has to come from somewhere, so there's a brisk business in which individuals purchase land not for its farm value necessarily (although that may be an added benefit) but for the *rights to the water that's underneath that land.* And that's a great investment simply because the water generally gets replenished during rainy seasons.

For example, in mountainous Colorado, the aquifers get recharged pretty constantly, which means that the property that is underneath a farm also gets recharged, so the water is a renewable resource. The water that is consumable can be sold. The individual who makes that investment in those water rights gets a contract (perpetual rider) or some kind of a lease pertaining to that particular water. The nature of the contract depends on the particular situation.

Water rights leaseholders can either sell the leases to private individuals, or they can sell them to government agencies. We know many cases in which people have sold the private water rights that they've purchased under land that they've owned directly to a government agency. First they bought the land, and then they purchased the water rights associated with it.

Not only do the water aquifers continue to be recharged, unlike other resources such as gas and oil, which are gone after they've been consumed, but other sources for power are available; there is no alternative that people can use as a substitute for water. People need water for growing food and personal consumption. However, there's still a challenge with a restored or renewed resource, such as water, in places where the local population is so high that the ability to produce water does not keep pace with people's use. So in addition to investing in water rights investments, you might want to consider investing in water projects for developing consumable water supplies, such as the facilities under construction in China and India. Of particular importance are areas that are becoming deserts, such as sub-Saharan Africa, where the Sahara deserts are continuing to expand into the rest of Africa at a fairly alarming pace. The people who live in these regions need water, but it's becoming a difficult resource to obtain. Investing in projects that promote obtaining water from ground sources or other places for everyday consumption as well as agriculture purposes is a good long-term approach.

How to Find Opportunities for Investing in Natural Resources

To research possible investing opportunities, the easiest way is through the Internet. Type in the search terms "water rights" or "water projects," and you'll get numerous hits. Of course, you need to make sure that you're not investing in, as the old scam goes, swampland in Florida or the Brooklyn Bridge. The best way to avoid being scammed is to focus on what's local to you. To protect yourself and invest safely, try as much as possible to deal with people you know or to visit the places that interest you—that is, to physically go and look at each project—to ensure that they really exist.

For example, we first became aware of investing in water rights because we got a call at our company, Entrust, in 1996, from a guy in Wyoming who wanted us to help him invest $50,000 from his IRA in water rights. Just out of curiosity, we asked him—his name is Bruce—how he found out about this opportunity. Bruce said, "I've been working for the water department for the last 30 years, so I know where the water is. And I can buy these water rights from a private rancher for 50 grand, and I know that I'll be able to sell it to the federal government for about $2 million." Obviously, that caught our attention.

At first, we were concerned that this was an insider deal, but Bruce assured us it wasn't. He said, "I just know that the government's going to need to supply water to all these people by a federal government fiat, and I know about that because I have access to the information"—which was publicly available. He continued to explain how this deal would work. "It's really simple. The Department of Interior tells you what kinds of contracts and what kinds of requirements it has to find the resource, how to acquire it, and where to sell it. Then, there are requests for proposals (RFPs) and contracts that you can enter into with the government. The government will offer you a deal, along the lines of 'I will buy your water for x number of dollars because I need it for such-and-such a purpose,' whether it's a reclamation, hydroelectric, or some other type of project."

So that's how Bruce found out about this opportunity. We thought it was very interesting, yet it took a year to work out the details of how he could make this investment via his IRA because we had to make sure that the purchase was done correctly and properly. And sure enough, just as Bruce had projected, he made a couple of million dollars on his $50,000 investment. As an aside, he converted his traditional IRA to a Roth IRA, which wasn't introduced until 1998. This was another reason it took a year to finalize the deal. We wanted to wait for the Roth to go into effect. The advantage to taxpayers is that Roth IRA money is after-tax dollars, so you never pay tax again on that money.

Bruce isn't the only person, of course, who has made a lot of money investing in water rights. And you don't have to be in the water business for 30 years to find out about these opportunities. All you really need to do is be open to alternative investing ideas and be on the lookout for new ways to invest.

After we helped Bruce invest in water rights through his IRA in 1998, we ran into him about six years later at a real estate conference that we were sponsoring in San Francisco. We were with one of our instructors, Jen Disning, and Bruce showed up. We were just about to introduce him to Jen when Bruce said, "Hugh made me rich." (Hugh had helped Bruce structure his investment through his Roth IRA.) Jen belongs to several investment clubs in Fort Collins, Colorado. She is very gregarious and enjoys talking to people. So at one of the investment clubs, she was chatting with an attorney (we'll call him Bob). She mentioned that she had met Bruce: "I met this guy from Wyoming who made a fortune in water rights. Sounds like an interesting idea." Bob responded, "Hey, I happen to be in that business too, here in Colorado."

What Bob is doing in Colorado is acquiring an interest in farms and ranches to use the water underneath it. He is then selling the water rights to other people, such as ranchers or public utilities districts. He is essentially a water broker. He recognizes that the demand for water is always going to be there because people need water, plain and simple. Places go through droughts, and people need to consume water. Bob has investors outside of Colorado in places all over the world. For example, he even sells to a big investor from India who is always looking to buy water rights in the United States.

Initially, Jen invested about $10,000 through Bob. Since then, she has invested up to about $100,000, generally in $10,000 increments. There isn't really a minimum investment (as you often find with other types of investments). However, $10,000 doesn't really go very far when you're buying water rights because these solo providers, who are local landowners and farmers, are often looking for a couple of hundred thousand dollars. Although, in the overall scheme of things, that's not a lot of money for a particular project or piece of property. Bob pools people's money and gives them a share of interest in the pool. Bob buys property with that pool of money, and then he buys the rights to the water underneath the property. The good news is that in four years, Jen has tripled her money.

Due Diligence When Investing in Natural Resources

So how do you find opportunities like these? The best thing to do is to get involved with the people who are into water—for example, community water districts. These local agencies are a good starting place to find out what the demands are in that community for water, as well as what the community's master plan is for ensuring water supply and reclamation. Then you should start looking for what water resources are available to meet that particular demand or what the community's plans are to meet that demand. If, let's say, a government water district has a particular requirement, you can follow the trail of where the water is supposed to come from.

On a private basis, if individual ranchers or farmers in the United States need water and they don't have it from an upstream environment, that is a more complicated investment situation than dealing with a government agency. Farmers tend to be very smart and resourceful, and they've usually already looked for their own resources. They're not going to need to buy water rights from you after you've bought them from someone else.

However, when you go outside of the United States, people aren't that savvy, and there are lots of programs and countries (which you can find through the United Nations) where water is a limited resource in high demand. But just because there is a high demand for a limited amount of water and there are opportunities for buying and selling water rights, it doesn't mean the deals are easy to make. Investing in water rights in other countries is a lot trickier than it is in the United States, so you need to visit the site that you're considering investing in to be sure that there really is water in that location.

The sub-Sahara region in Africa is a really good example. The people who live there are trying to find drinking water. So is that a good investment? Maybe, but maybe not because all they're really doing is digging wells. They aren't developing new water supplies, but just tapping into their existing aquifer. However, in these situations, you might instead invest in the companies that are in the well-digging business. In other words, you should look at ancillary businesses surrounding the water sources located in these particular areas.

You don't *have* to travel to Africa to visit the location you're considering investing in. However, one of the things that we've discovered during our years of experience in investing in many different things is that the more familiar you become with *any* kind of an investment opportunity, the better off you'll be. If you take the time and effort to visit a location, if you become completely familiar with it, you're going to have a much better chance of success than somebody who didn't. Individuals can give you a prospectus that says what they're going to do, but you really don't know whether that prospectus is accurate unless you verify it. That's one of the risks of investing in alternative investments, and it's part of the reason people get burned: They can't or don't do the due diligence. *Due diligence is really important,* no matter what investment you're considering. So again, you don't *have* to visit the site. But if you're going to invest in a company that is going to be digging wells in the sub-Sahara, you want to first make sure that there is a demand for water and, second, that this company is actually drilling wells and providing water, and finally, that they're going to get paid for it.

In Jen's case, after she met Bob the water broker, she knew she needed to do due diligence on Bob's operations to make sure that he was really on the up and up. First, she asked him to tell her everything about his plans and everything he knew about the water situation in the region in which he was planning to buy water rights—which was in the Rocky Mountains in Colorado. Then, because Jen had been a broker and a real estate investor, she knew she needed to look at the actual deals Bob was making. Because she lived in Colorado, she was able to physically look at the property that he was buying. She determined that there was indeed water underneath it, that there was a way to get to the water, and that the water was going to be sold to somebody else. (And she did this on each of the deals in which she later invested.)

After she visited the land, it was obvious that it wasn't a desert because there were plants growing on it, which of course meant that there was water underneath. Bob was pumping out of the aquifers, which are recharged by rainwater. This was critical for her to see for herself because someone could buy a piece of land that doesn't have any water underneath it (the water needs to be anywhere from a hundred feet to several thousand feet underneath). You have to know where the water is. You don't need to be a geologist or have a geology degree to determine this because the people who are in the water rights business hire geologists, and Jen was able to talk to them. Of course, there's still the possibility that you could be dealing with a con artist who has hired someone to pose as a geologist, but in this case, Jen saw that Bob's company was indeed pumping water and selling it to buyers. Also in this case, Jen could tell by talking to the geologist that he had done a subterranean investigation. He was also able to present maps and other documents, indicating that he knew what he was doing. Another good indicator that there's water on a property is if there's a windmill on top, or if there's a pump with a well underneath it and water is coming out. So you know there's water, although you don't know how much.

Then the science comes into play. If you're doing your due diligence and you can see that there's water coming out of the ground, you need to determine whether the water is usable or potable. If it's not, you can get burned. For example, in the Central Valley in California, people have bought farms that they could never grow anything on because they don't have economical access to the right type of water. There are different kinds of water, and they're used for different purposes. For example, salt water must be desalinized to use as drinking water or farm irrigation. So you need to determine the *purpose and usability* of the water that you're going to invest in. That's as important as getting the water itself.

The importance of due diligence cannot be overstated. For example, here's one sad story of some people who got burned by buying land that had water under it but the land was still not usable. Many of the Vietnamese who came to the United States after the fall of Saigon in 1975 were farmers. They moved to the California Central Valley because it seemed to be rich in farmland. Unfortunately, some less-than-scrupulous people were selling land and took advantage of the Vietnamese farmers in the guise of giving them a "good deal." The farmers thought the land looked great, so they bought it with the idea of digging a well to get the water they needed to grow their crops.

Unfortunately, the land these unscrupulous dealers sold to the farmers had been completely salted by the previous owners. As land is used, any chemicals or salts applied to it stay on the surface because they don't evaporate. No matter how much water you put on that land, all you would end up with is salty earth. You could have an abundance of water, but you still couldn't grow anything because the land would become a giant salt marsh. This is an example of why it's *so critical* to do extensive due diligence—you must know *exactly* what you're buying.

The salt could have been washed out by mechanical means, but that is a very expensive process, and it was way beyond the financial means of the Vietnamese farmers. In this specific case, the biggest disadvantage these immigrants had was that, even though they were very knowledgeable about productive farms in their own country, they had no local contacts in the Central Valley who could help them communicate not only with the people who were selling the land but with experts in local agriculture. That's why we believe it's so important to visit (if it's at all possible) the locations you're considering investing in so that you can talk to the local people and to educate yourself as much as you can before you invest a single dollar in anything.

The worst story that we know of someone not doing due diligence and getting burned does not involve investing in natural resources but it concerns investigating all that you can. We had a number of clients of Entrust who were extremely interested in investing in mobile cell phone towers with a company called Dallas MobileCom. Our clients were interested because the Dallas MobileCom people—who are now in jail—were saying, "We are going to be at the forefront of communications in Texas. We're building 20 towers across the state in the most important areas where people want to communicate with their cell phones." This was back around 1992, in the very early days of cell phones when they were still big and heavy and clunky. In fact, this is when they were still called car phones because they really weren't a practical size to carry around. But people had begun investing their money in this technology.

For about two or three years, Dallas MobileCom had been promoting itself to potential investors. We then got a call from the attorneys for the secretary of state in Texas. The attorneys told us that there were some questions surrounding whether or not Dallas MobileCom would be able to develop these towers. Of course, we found that very interesting and very important in terms of our clients who wanted to invest in this company.

So we started asking questions, like where are the towers? This is exactly what we've been emphasizing throughout this book—that before you invest in anything, you need to talk to the people at the companies you're considering investing in, and you need to physically find out whether those people have actually developed anything. In this case, Dallas MobileCom simply answered, "Well, they're not up yet." If you can't physically point to something that you've built or developed, *it's not real*—at least not yet.

Unfortunately, many people did invest in Dallas MobileCom, and we couldn't prevent them from doing so because in our business at Entrust, we can't give anybody advice, pro or con, about any investment. All we could do in this case was tell our clients to call the secretary of state's office in Texas and ask them about it, and that's what we did. And what the secretary of state's office told people who called was this: "This guy has only two weeks left to build 20 towers, and he hasn't started a single one, and he's got $16 million of other people's money."

Sure enough, the two weeks went by, and none of the cell towers had been built. So the owner of Dallas Mobile-Com was arrested and thrown in jail. But the $16 million had already gone to an offshore account, so the money was, for all intents and purposes, gone. Everybody who had invested in his company lost all their money. They had invested because he had great brochures and slick promotional materials, and none of the investors had bothered asking any questions.

We had one client in Louisiana who had just taken his rollover money—$425,000—out of his Shell Oil retirement account and had put it into an IRA. He wanted to invest it in Dallas MobileCom. This was at the end of this company's scam, when we knew from talking to the secretary of state's office that this was not going to happen, that this company was not going to be able to build 20 cell towers in two weeks. So we called our client and explained, "Look, we can't tell you what to do with your money. We have to obey your directions, but we would like you to do some due diligence." We felt it was rather reckless for him to take all of his retirement money and invest it in just this one thing. So he took our advice, and he called the secretary of state's office and spoke to the attorney we had referred him to. Then he called us back because he still wanted to invest his money in the cell towers. We asked him if he had talked to the attorney at the secretary of state's office, and he said that he had. When we asked what he had told him, he said, "You know the government. They don't want you to make any money." We later found out that the attorney at the secretary of state's office had indeed told our client that there was no way that Dallas MobileCom could deliver on what it was promising because it had to build 20 towers in two weeks. Unfortunately, our client trusted the cell tower con artist more than he trusted the government office.

So what does that tell you? There's a fool born every minute, and our client was one of them: He lost his entire retirement fund of $425,000. After he discovered that his investment had completely crashed, he called us back and said, "Well, I lost all my money, so I guess I'm going to be fishing for crayfish in the Bayous. I've got a little farm down here, and I'll just do the best I can." He did have a marvelous attitude about losing all of this retirement money.

The government can't arrest someone if a crime hasn't been committed. It wasn't until Dallas MobileCom failed to build the cell towers that the government could arrest the owner and put him in jail. So in this case, all we could do is warn our investors and encourage them to research this opportunity further by actually going to Texas and looking for the cell towers. But many people don't want to do this because there's work and time and money involved. Yet when you're going to invest in new businesses or alternative opportunities, we can't emphasize enough that *you need to do your due diligence.*

Don't get burned the way our client did. You might not have his good attitude when you lose all your money and realize you need to work until you're dead. There are plenty of con artists, particularly in hard times, because they need to make money too. They'll steal every penny you have because they have no conscience. Don't let that happen to you.

Due Diligence in Relation to the Size of Your Investment

Due diligence is absolutely critical when you're considering any type of investing—even buying bonds or investing in the S&P 500. However, you also need to consider how much due diligence you *can* feasibly do and how much you're *willing* to do. Those factors often depend on the amount of money you're considering investing in any particular opportunity.

For example, suppose you have $10,000 to invest. Frankly, that's not a lot of money to invest, so you have to limit what you're going to invest in. With $10,000, you might get a good return by simply investing in publicly listed securities (that is, the stock market) and hope that those investments work for you. For instance, you could buy stock in the Coca-Cola Company, which is a fairly safe investment because you know Coke is sold all over the world. You do not have to go to Atlanta to visit the Coca-Cola headquarters and see how Coke is made and bottled and marketed and sold to determine whether buying stock in the company is a good idea. So that investment should make you really comfortable, and you're probably not going to get burned, unless you don't know anything about Coca-Cola. That, of course, is the Warren Buffett approach: He invests only in what he knows.

Although Warren Buffett is a good role model and certainly a successful investor, his risk profile is very different from yours and ours. He can toss a few million bucks away, and it wouldn't make any difference to his overall wealth, which was recently estimated at $50 billion. But if you have only $10,000 to invest, then $1,000 is a lot of money to you, and you wouldn't want to lose 10 percent of your investment. So if you're a $10,000 investor, you have to be extremely careful about how you manage your money. You need to know exactly what you want to do with it, you need to know how to use it in the best way, and you need to decide how much time and effort you're going to spend doing your due diligence on potential investments. All of those factors limit what you're going to invest in.

That's also why it's important to focus on investment opportunities that are *local to you*. You should invest in something that *you* know, with people whom you know you can trust in terms of their decision-making capabilities regarding what they invest in or the advice that they give you. In Jen Disning's case, she got to know and trust Bob the water broker. As mentioned, her initial investments were $10,000. But she had enormous power with her $10,000 because she invested in a local water broker, and she could see what he could do. She could drive out to the property that was being purchased, see the water being produced, and see where that water was going. That research didn't cost her a heck of a lot of money. She did spend a lot of time, and time is really the most valuable commodity we have, but Jen's investment of time was reasonable. The company she was considering was local, so the amount of time she spent was relatively low in relation to the amount of gain she hoped to have from her investment.

On the other hand, if your $10,000 is the only money you have to invest with, and there isn't a natural resource that's local to you, or if you're not interested in whatever investing opportunities are local to you, you can still decide to invest in a company like Chevron (or any other publicly traded company). Then the only due diligence you need to do is to look at the company's balance sheet to make sure that it is not collapsing, going bankrupt, or making silly investments.

Just as an aside, what happened globally in 2008 was that people and banks thought they had an iron-clad, wonderful deal when they invested in mortgage-backed securities. But neither the individual investors nor the banks had done their due diligence, so they failed to understand that all the people who had gotten those subprime mortgages weren't going to be able to pay them off. These were multibillion-dollar companies who made these bad investments because they chose not to do their due diligence and understand the deals they were investing in.

So now you need to do due diligence even on companies like Coca-Cola or any other publicly traded company so that you can make sure you know what *they're* investing in and what type of deals they're involved in. Even if you're not buying mortgage-backed securities directly (or other equally risky investments), you need to make sure that whatever company or entity you *are* investing in won't end up collapsing, as did so many companies and banks and other institutions in recent years. Because large companies tend to be global, they tend to invest in things that we—the average investors—often have no idea about. Sometimes we can examine their balance sheets and see what risks these companies have assumed. Then we can make our own judgments about whether we feel comfortable about whatever Coca-Cola, for example, is investing in. *You simply have to do that.* If all you have is $10,000, you can't afford to lose $10,000. If you have $1 billion and you lose $10 million, that's not a lot of money to lose. I'm sure that billionaires hate to lose $10 million because that money would buy a nice part of a jet or something, but it's not the end of the world for them.

But if you have only $10,000, or even $100,000, to invest, and that's *all* the money you have, you need to invest that money in something that you're not going to get burned in, that has a net operating income that's going to make you happy and meet your investing goals and objectives on a long-term basis, and that requires you to pay the lowest possible taxes that you can legally get away with.

How to Research Possible Investments

So how do you find possible investments in natural resources? Essentially (and as with most other alternative investing opportunities described in this book), there are two feasible ways to do this for smaller investors. One way is to join an investment club (as Jen Disning did) and talk to a lot of investors who are involved in many different types of investments. Investment clubs are a great way to find out about different opportunities and to network among people you know and trust and who have actually had success and failure with a variety of investments.

The other way is to spend hours and hours in the dark on your computer, researching Web sites, getting information, reading prospectuses, and reviewing balance sheets. As we've emphasized throughout the book, due diligence requires researching and getting as much information as you can about whatever investing opportunity intrigues you. Investing in anything, but especially in things outside your primary business and life experience, requires you to get an enormous amount of basic knowledge. For instance, unless you're a geologist or have the 30 years' experience working for the water department that Bruce had before he bought water rights in Wyoming, you must educate yourself in these areas.

Fortunately, an abundance of information is available on the Internet and in books. However, we recommend that you not just read but also try to talk to people who know about what you're considering investing in. Then you can make an intelligent decision about the investment based on your personal risk comfort level. To make your investment, you're going to be writing a check or sending a wire transfer to a corporation or other entity. Make sure that you're sending your hard-earned money to a real corporation or entity and that you're investing in a piece of property that you *know* exists.

Investing in Oil and Gas

People have been investing in gas and oil for decades. The price of oil fluctuates considerably over the short term—for example, in 2008, it hit a high in the $140s per barrel, and in June 2009 it went down to $70. Oil exploration will continue to be a great place for people to invest. As we've seen, even though the price of oil will continue to fluctuate over short terms, it will go up over time.

Investing in oil as an alternative investment means investing in the small companies that are in the exploration business, instead of the giant oil companies like Chevron, where, if you want to invest, you simply buy stock in the company—that is, you make a more traditional investment. For example, Reef Securities is a company that many Entrust clients have invested in. One part of its business is in oil exploration and another is in development. Businesses generally pursue both oil and gas interests because where oil is found, gas is often found. There are also "dry wells"—wells that don't have oil but do have water—which people sometimes invest in. However, because dry wells don't have any oil production capability, those investments don't pay off very well.

When the oil exploration results in discovering oil, gas, or water, it is placed into a production cycle. The cost of production depends on the prevailing wellhead price for the oil, gas, or water at that time. An example of how this cost relationship works can be seen in what happened in 2008. Prior to 2008, many individual small companies had effectively closed their wells down because the cost of producing oil was higher than the price of oil in the oil markets. Obviously, when the cost of production is less than the selling price of a barrel of oil—in other words, when the oil producers can make a profit when they sell their oil to a refinery—these small companies can put those oil wells back into production. And that's a big business, and it'll probably stay a big business in the United States for a long period of time.

Having said that, the United States has only 2 percent of the world's proven reserves of oil—that's all that's left in the United States. However, the United States also produces 45 percent of its own oil requirements. Many people don't know that, but it is important because the United States will eventually run out of oil. That's why Chevron, Exxon Mobil, and other big oil companies around the world have now gotten into alternative energy sources. When oil runs out, they will have to develop in places outside the United States or seek alternative energy sources.

If you're willing to do the necessary due diligence to find alternative investing opportunities in oil and gas exploration, there are many oil and gas LLCs that you can invest in. In general, these are "small" companies, but they still do a lot of business. These companies are in the neighborhood of $10 million in terms of what their requirements are to do the exploration and production. Fortunately, *you* don't need $10 million. You can invest as little as $10,000 in these smaller companies.

So how can you find these smaller exploration companies? You can, of course, search on the Internet simply by Googling "oil exploration." That's really the best place to start your research. There are also dozens of good periodicals that you can find on the Web or at your local library. For example:

- *American Oil & Gas Reporter*: www.aogr.com
- *Aspermont Oil & Gas*: www.ozoilgas.com
- *Hart's E&P Net*: www.EandPnet.com
- *Offshore Magazine*: www.offshore-mag.com
- *Oil & Gas Business Journal*: www.ogbus.com
- *Oil & Gas Eurasia*: www.oilandgaseurasia.com
- *Oil & Gas Financial Journal*: www.ojg.com
- *Oil & Gas Journal*: www.ojg.com
- *Oil & Gas Petrochem Equipment*: www.ojg.com

In these periodicals, you can easily find companies that interest you. Then you can simply call them and start talking to people who work for them, which is a great way to educate yourself and get the information you need to start making sound investments.

We know many people who have invested in oil and gas exploration. Moreover, we've done it ourselves, starting in 1981 and continuing on and off over the years. We like investing in oil because we know that oil is a finite resource. After you consume a barrel of oil and liberate the energy from it, it's gone, and there isn't any new oil being made on this planet. We started investing in oil in 1981 because we were looking for tax credits. We asked Gordon, our CPA (who is also a financial planner), if he had any ideas, and he said, "I've got a great deal in oil and gas for you. Not only can you make income on this but you will also get a tax credit, which will diminish the amount you have to pay in taxes, resulting in more spendable money for you." Of course, we thought that was a wonderful idea, so we invested $25,000, which was a lot of money in 1981, but we thought it was a sound investment.

Financial planners are a wonderful resource for finding various kinds of investments. They generally get some kind of payment from a company—like the oil and gas exploration companies we invested in—to which they refer investors. When financial planners or advisors are getting a referral fee for the investment, they are required to disclose that fee to you.

In terms of due diligence, we didn't need to do any due diligence on Gordon because he was a neighbor in our office suite, and he had been highly recommended through a banker we worked with. We found him through networking. We trusted Gordon because he did all the tax returns and handled investments for several bankers we worked with, and all of those bankers were pleased with the work he had done for them. Also, back in 1981, although we were young and naïve, fortunately, working with Gordon and investing in the oil exploration company he suggested worked out for us. Since then, a lot of other people have not done as well because they were given bad advice. Many of the investments that some financial planners intended to be tax credits were ultimately disallowed, and a lot of people ended up paying a lot more in taxes than they had planned.

Therefore, when you find an oil and gas company that you are interested to invest in, we recommend that you contact the company. Get all the information that the company is willing to share with you and *read it thoroughly*. If the company offers presentations, go to its presentations and ask hard questions about everything you've gleaned from its prospectus. Fortunately, these days, prospectuses (even for companies that are not publicly traded) are very informative, and they tell you all of the downsides (as well as the upsides, of course). At the company's presentations, you can ask the company's representatives hard questions in the presence of other people. Other people will want the same information you're looking for, and you'll get a fuller answer in a public forum than you would in a one-on-one conversation. You'll also learn from the questions that other people ask.

After you've read the prospectus and all the other information that the company has given you, determine what the upsides and downsides are *for you to invest* at that particular time. Companies are required to tell you what their *actual* returns are, so make sure you get the actual returns, not estimated or projected returns. There are people and companies out there that inflate their returns and say "You can make this kind of a return" when there's really nothing to back up that claim and when that estimate will become real only if everything goes well. People who are selling something want to tell you that you're getting the best deal. But you have to look at it *from your personal point of view* and whether or not they're just giving you their best guess or hope of how the exploration and production will take place.

What you really want to know is whether or not the company has a production facility. Are they really producing oil? If they're developing oil or gas, are they really developing? Of course, we didn't know this in 1981. As mentioned, we simply trusted Gordon, our CPA and financial planner, and we were fortunate that our investment paid off. We made 12 percent gross, and that was with the tax credits, so it was close to net, which was a great return. Also, we knew it was all legal and above board. We were very fortunate because Gordon was indeed an honest guy, and we are good friends to this day, almost 30 years later. But over the years, we've become increasingly skeptical because we've met too many people who have said "We're doing oil and gas exploration," after which we've discovered that they weren't doing oil and gas exploration at all. Instead, they were running Ponzi schemes.

There are investment advisors who have steered people into oil and gas investments that have been bogus. Even the investment advisors get approached by these con artists, and they don't necessarily know themselves whether they're real. So registered investment advisors—RIAs must be registered with the SEC—might recommend something in good faith but fail to do their own due diligence and get burned as a result. You need to trust the people you get advice from. But even after you get advice, you must make sure that what you're investing in is a good investment. Plenty of small reputable companies are generating good returns for their investors, but you still need to be thorough in your due diligence.

How We Did Due Diligence on an Oil Exploration Investment

Back in 2003, we invested in an oil exploration company that we were able to check out by visiting one of its production operations. We found out about this company during a presentation that the company gave at a conference sponsored by Robert Kiyosaki, the author of *Rich Dad, Poor Dad*. We've known Robert for over 10 years, and we know he does a lot of due diligence, so we're confident that he won't get involved with anybody or invest in anything that's not completely reliable. The company's presentation was very informative, so we got to know the principals and their salespeople. They were willing to talk to people individually, which was very reassuring.

They also provided education in terms of what to look for in oil and gas production, which was one of the reasons we liked this company. They didn't just try to sell people on investing in their particular company. Like many other companies looking for investors, they had a road show during which they were willing to answer questions such as "Where are you exploring?"; "What do you see in the future for this industry?"; "How do you explore?"; "How do you develop?"; "What are the relationships between costs and prices?" And they gave the specifics and details about where their exploration was taking place and how it worked.

They had two different companies—one that did exploration and another that did development—so you could invest in either or both. We were given the location of all of their sites (which was in stark contrast to Dallas MobileCom, the cell tower company we described earlier in the chapter that didn't have any actual sites because it hadn't built any cell towers with the $16 million the owner had collected from various investors). We could visit these sites and see where they were doing their oil and gas exploration.

In terms of exploration, instead of drilling in new areas, the company was buying old oil fields that were no longer producing or deemed nonproductive at one time. The company would then intelligently assess each of the sites as to whether it was worthwhile to drill deeper and longer. The company's thinking was that if an area used to be productive, it could be productive again. The decision to drill would depend on the relationship of cost and price. For example, when oil was $11 a barrel, it wasn't worthwhile to keep drilling a well that was not producing. But when the oil price was $60 a barrel—or $140, as the prices were during the high of 2008—it was worthwhile.

A lot of oil fields in California have Henry wells, which are the oil pumps that look like a bird's beak going up and down. None of those are running when the price of oil is low, but they start running when the price of oil goes up because the energy required to pump out a few barrels or a few hundred barrels is cost effective. Many of these production facilities are owned by smaller companies, not by the giants like Exxon Mobil. These smaller companies might sell their oil to the big oil companies, but they're not owned by them. And it's these smaller companies that buy up older oil fields because, even if they produce only 50 barrels a day, it can be cost effective to run them when the price of oil is high.

Anyway, back to due diligence. As mentioned, we were intrigued by this company, which provided detailed and specific information on where it was drilling. One of its locations was in Louisiana, which is a major oil-producing region. The company had offshore facilities, and we were able to visit them. The company gave us a map of where its production facilities were, and we went to some of the sites to see whether the facilities really existed. At one site we saw a drill rig, where the company had purchased the rights to drill. A couple dozen people were working there to make sure that everything was continuing to operate on a regular basis.

We also talked to some of the workers, including the supervisor of the production facility, for about 15 minutes. We asked a few questions about what they were doing. They told us they were part of a consortium, which a few people had bought into. They mentioned that they handled only the drilling and the pumping and that they had nothing to do with the investment aspects of the site development and operation. Of course, we didn't tell them we were potential investors; we led them to believe we were tourists. We felt comfortable talking to the workers because, back in the 1980s, Hugh had done some consulting work for Shell Oil, so we knew a little about oil exploration and production—enough, at least, to ask intelligent questions.

The answers the oil rig workers gave us satisfied us that, first, there was a rig; second, the rig was producing oil for a number of investors; and third, the oil was being sold to the major oil companies and other customers. That was all we really needed to know. We had wanted to visit the drill rig so that we could see for ourselves that these people were real, that they had real equipment, and that they had a real infrastructure. We wanted to do what our client that we mentioned earlier, the client that had invested in Dallas MobileCom, failed to do: He never went to Texas to see if Dallas MobileCom had actually built any cell phone towers. If that client had done his due diligence, he would have seen that those towers never existed. In contrast, we were willing to do the necessary due diligence, and we saw that the oil exploration company existed and that it had a working rig.

The company's returns were published as they were required to be by the government. We were able to look at those as well as the company's production data, which was reasonably trustworthy. We could assess the company's track record, and when we did so, we realized that this was a really good deal. Because of all the research we did, we were ready to make an investment. We believed that the demand for oil would either remain flat or increase. Since the supply of oil is relatively scarce, the prospects were good for our investment. We knew the company was in the hands of reputable people. All these factors combined led us to decide that the income we would make on our investment was where we would like it to be—that on a long-term basis (in our case, 10 to 20 years because we take the long view of investing), this company was going to make us money.

After we came back from Louisiana, we also talked to other people who had invested in this company. Some of our clients at Entrust had already invested, so we were able to check the oil company's references. Their positive responses added to our comfort level, so we invested the next time the company was looking for investors. The company was opening and closing different projects at different times. When it was starting a new exploration project, it would determine how much money it needed to obtain from investors. Then it would use that money to fund the project's production and exploration. The company operated its finances similar to the way the retail industry operates when it is in an open-to-buy situation and retailers are ready to buy new merchandise for their stores.

If investors are happy with the results of one project and if everything went well, they're likely to invest in another one, which is what we did. So we were actually investing in specific development or production projects rather than investing in the company itself. We liked the fact that our investments were project specific, because we knew what we were gaining or losing on each particular exploration project. Essentially, we were diversifying our investments within this particular area. If one of the projects we had invested in turned out to be a loser, we would not have lost all our money. By diversifying our investments among different oil exploration and development projects, we could use dollar-cost averaging. The probability was good that even if one project was a total loser, another project would be a real winner. The more you can diversify into different projects, the better off you are.

In addition, we didn't invest one lump sum at one time. Rather, we invested different amounts over four years or so. When you diversify your investments in different projects, you have many more opportunities to succeed because the amount of investment per project can be relatively low. For example, some projects require a $5,000 investment, whereas others require $50,000 each. Your investment decisions center on what you want to do and how much you want to invest at any one time.

We invested in $10,000 increments, and we made about 20 percent overall on our investments with this company. Of course, some of our $10,000 investments returned nothing, so we were happy that we had diversified because of the gamble involved. Even though some exploration projects didn't produce any oil, they did produce by-products like water that could be sold, so we didn't lose all of our money in those investments. Finding water as a by-product of gas and oil well production does not always produce a clear-cut gain for an investor. Our investments with this particular company proved to be educational for us because we discovered that there's good water and there's bad water. Sometimes, the company found sweet water, but other times it found arsenic or alkaline water, neither of which can be used for drinking. Other aspects of water well operations affected the profitability of our investments. For example, the worth of the water depended on where the well was located. The company could sell the water to consumers only if the water was both usable and close to where the consumers needed it. Typically, water is not what people are looking for when they're exploring for oil.

In addition, this company was a good investing opportunity because it didn't buy just a single well — it bought many previously dormant wells. By buying an area that had a lot of wells, the company was also diversifying and distributing its risk among many opportunities.

Finally, if somebody contacts you and says, "Hey, I've got a deal for you: I'm digging a well now, and I know it's a surefire well," you do not want to invest in that. That just ain't going to happen. There is the remote possibility that someone may find somewhere in the United States more oil than there is in Saudi Arabia, but the likelihood is next to nothing that that's going to happen. So investor, beware! And do your due diligence.

INVESTING IN BIOFUELS

The last area of natural resources that we want to touch on is of great interest to the general public right now: biofuels. Biofuels are derived from agricultural products such as corn and sugarcane that can be used to produce ethanol. In the United States, sugarcane is not as popular as corn for producing ethanol. Sugarcane is harvested for ethanol mostly in Brazil, which is a major producer of biofuel.

Biofuels fit into the category of renewable resources. They can be used to power motor vehicles, including cars. The result is that we can use these fuels to replace some of the oil we currently use for that purpose. Although biofuels are not as efficient as oil fuels in terms of production and the energy biofuels produce is different from that produced by oil, they can still replace some of the oil we presently use. So this is a huge market.

Processing biofuels also generates huge quantities of many useful by-products. For example, one of the by-products of biodiesel production is glycerin, which is a major component in soap and cosmetic products. Another by-product is feed for dairy cows and cattle. So when you invest in biofuels, you can also earn a return on your investment from the by-products. The biofuel industry is growing steadily in the United States. If you're in an agricultural area, companies are probably producing it—which means you can invest in it—because they're able to get some money out of it as well as some money out of the by-products.

NatureWorks LLC in Minnesota is an example of a biofuel producing company. It is a joint venture with the Cargill and Teijin Limited company of Japan. NatureWorks is using by-products from ethanol production to make polymers, which are then used to make stuffing for pillows and comforters, shrink-wrap, carpets, and even clothes. Because this company is an LLC, it's still small enough that people can invest in it. We have clients at Entrust who have invested in NatureWorks and that has led us to make investments in green businesses. NatureWorks is only one company pursuing green business; there are many others, including large companies, such as DuPont. Of course, investing in DuPont is not an alternative investment: You simply buy stock in the company.

If you're interested in investing in green companies like NatureWorks, it's very easy to find them. You can search for them via the Internet, or you can ask about them from other investors at investor club meetings. Once you start looking and talking to people, you'll find many ancillary alternative investing opportunities. For example, if you start looking for biofuels, you'll discover biomaterials, which are plastics (or bioplastics). You'll find many other amazing potential investments surrounding the biofuel industries. If you're into green and clean, alternative investment opportunities are growing up all over the place, resulting not only from biofuel production itself but also from its production by-products.

You can also look at the rather large companies that use the outputs of biofuels, for example, Honda and Toyota. Toyota is expecting to use 20 million tons of bioplastic over the next decade and a half. Toyota manufactures the Prius hybrid car, so if that continues to sell well, Toyota will need to find more sources of bioplastics. And that might be a good alternative investing opportunity.

CHAPTER

SOCIALLY RESPONSIBLE GREEN INVESTING
Solar, Wind, and Wave Power

In this chapter, we cover socially responsible investing, focusing on investing in alternatives to nonrenewable energy resources. The green side of this topic is that solar, wind, and wave power leave a very small carbon footprint— that is, these power sources generate very small amounts of greenhouse gas emissions. They do not cause ecological damage directly (although, of course, the manufacture of anything always has some impact on the environment). From the point of view of fuel replacement, using solar, wind, and wave power reduces dependence on fossil fuels, which are expensive and will become more so. Solar, wind, and wave power are usually local enterprises, so using them also reduces dependence on foreign oil supplies, which in turn reduces the impact of international oil trade on geopolitical situations.

Investing in Solar Power

We first got involved with investing in solar power in 2006 as part of a small community action project in San Rafael, California. Some homeowners in this community wanted to install solar panels on their rooftops to generate solar energy to be used primarily in their own homes. This particular tract has 508 homes and generally million-dollar homes, so the homeowners had some means. The community organizer was one of the homeowners named Harry. Harry had a passion for solar power and had done a lot of preliminary investigation, and he wanted to get this community involved.

Harry had no financial vested interest in people using solar power for their homes. He wasn't going to make any money if people in the community chose to buy solar power equipment nor was he interested in benefiting financially from selling any excess power generated by the homeowners. He simply wanted people to consider using solar power for its environmental benefits. He contacted each company that provided solar power panels and installations, and he asked each of them to make presentations to the community on their products and services. Surprisingly, there was a huge amount of interest, and about 100 families were represented in the first meeting. The individual homeowners then decided on whether they wished to pursue this technology and, if so, which providers they wanted to choose for their own properties.

Typically, solar power equipment and installation is a cash-and-carry business. However, in this community, some of the homeowners asked, "What if we want to finance the $30,000 cost of doing this?" The answer was that they could indeed finance it through third-party financing from people (like us) who essentially wanted to lend to the individuals who were installing the solar power in their homes. What we and other investors did was take a first or second deed of trust on a particular property that was going to have the solar power on it, and we lent the owners of those properties all or part of the money needed to install the solar power panels. That's how we originally got involved in it. You can find these opportunities by looking in your own backyard (metaphorically speaking). If you start asking around your community or your homeowners association, you can find people who need money, and you can help them via alternative investments.

One of the things we discovered was that investors could use their IRAs to do this, and a lot of people were very interested in that particular approach. That's how Entrust got involved. We had expertise in arranging for alternative investments via IRAs. As it turns out, solar power is probably going to be one of the major technologies that more and more people will be using to power their homes because solar power is effectively free power. All you have to do is amortize back the cost of the installation and hookup. The payback period is usually around 11 to 12 years on a typical home in California.

Just to clarify, we didn't invest in the solar power companies. You can buy stock in solar power companies, but that type of investment is not an alternative investment. Also, we weren't investing in the development of these homes, the way builders invest in new communities. Instead, the structure of our investments was based on the Uniform Commercial Code Form 1 (UCC-1), which is a particular kind of financing statement that allowed us (and any other investors) to secure the interest in the solar panels and, because they were attached to the houses, secure an interest in the houses as well.[1] The UCC-1 form is filed with the county recorder or the secretary of state's office, depending on the state in which the investment is located. The security interest in the property remains in effect until it is legally released.

When we filed these security forms, we gave the homeowners the money they needed to install their solar panels, and we had a security interest. Actually, in our case, our IRAs held the security interest. The individual homeowners paid back the loans. Of course, you do need to consider what would happen if a homeowner didn't pay back the loan. In our case, we (the investors) would get the house and the solar panels. In other words, the house had been put up as collateral.

Of the 100 homeowners who showed up at the initial meeting, 20 of them decided to switch to solar power and obtain financing from the four private investors. The size of the investments ranged from $12,000 to $30,000. We started these investments just two years ago. The loans are typically 10-year loans, and investors receive a monthly payment from each homeowner. In our case, we're getting 8 percent on these investments. We're satisfied with that rate of return because we know the investments are secure: We get the trust deed on the house, and that's a big deal. We know our risk is well mitigated because the house is securing it and because we know the homeowners. So far, it's going wonderfully. We're very pleased with the deal, and we would make this type of deal again any time.

---

[1] You can find the basic UCC-1 form on the Internet. The basic form is one page, but there is another one-page addendum and instructions for filling out both. If you don't use a lawyer to fill out the form, we recommend that you have your lawyer at least review it.

It's also a good deal from the homeowners' point of view. When they sell their houses with solar power capability, their houses will sell for a premium because having solar power is favorable to buyers. Home buyers realize that they won't have high energy costs.

INVESTING IN SOLAR POWER COMPANIES

The type of individual investing in solar power just described is obviously at the low end. The higher end is investing in solar companies themselves. Many solar companies are now owned by fairly large companies, including Chevron, Mitsubishi, and Sharp. It has become a big business. But smaller companies are also in the business of installing solar power capabilities, and you can still invest in small start-ups that are springing up practically every day.

We know of a few companies in California that are already a respectable size—for example, Borrego Solar, Prevalent Power, GoSolar Marin, SolarCity.com, and Real Good Solar (which installs and also provides the ability for homeowners to install their own). This list is just what's in Marin County, California. Solar companies are all over the country, so you can find investing opportunities in your own backyard.

Investing in small companies or start-ups falls under the general category of angel investing or venture capital investing. In these situations, you can invest anywhere from $10,000 to $50,000, $100,000, or $1 million. We know many people who have invested in companies like Borrego Solar, and their return is paid either through a note they've negotiated with the business or through owning a share of that business via a limited liability corporation (LLC). These investors have found companies like Borrego through their communities, because they're actively looking for alternative investments. We're near Silicon Valley, and entrepreneurs here are always coming up with new products—for instance, better chips that make collecting solar energy more efficient than ever before. These entrepreneurs are just like the stereotypical start-up in a garage, and they're pretty phenomenal. Some of them will likely go public at some point, but right now, they're private placements and small LLCs that people are investing in.

You can find many investment opportunities like this on the Internet. In our case, we've done the research, but we haven't yet invested in any start-ups. The only reason we haven't is that we've simply been too late on many of them. The companies we would have been interested in are already too well established. But if we could get in on the ground floor of a new company, we would invest.

Investing in Wind Power

Some very large players dominate wind power. Several Spanish and other European companies probably have the largest set of systems that use wind power. Stocks for these individual companies are available on various stock exchanges. Investors in countries other than the United States can invest more easily in these European companies because American investors can invest in them only via American Depositary Receipts (ADRs). (See Chapter 6 for more information on ADRs.)

Vestas is probably the single largest wind power company. According to its Web site (www.vestas.com), in 2009, Vestas promoted itself as the largest: "No. 1 in modern

energy, with a 20 percent market share, and 38,000 wind turbines installed, Vestas is the world's leading supplier of wind
power solutions." Headquartered in Denmark, the company
installed its first wind turbine in 1979, and it has grown to an
international company with 15,000 employees.

In contrast, the United States is just starting to get involved in building wind farms. The primary reason the
United States is slow is that we don't have the tax incentives to encourage the use of wind power that the Germans,
Danes, and Spanish have. Investors in those countries
don't have to worry about getting burned because the governments are providing incentives for individuals to make
these kinds of investments. These countries don't want to be
dependent on oil and natural gas, because these fuels are
supplied by Russia and other countries and transported via
pipelines. In contrast, the United States doesn't use much
fuel imported from Russia by pipeline. The United States
imports oil and natural gas via tankers, which is a more reliable means of shipment. So the United States does not feel
as much pressure to use alternative fuels such as wind and
tidal power.

One example of a publicly sanctioned tidal and wind
power generation plant is in Rhode Island. The state had
to give permission to the company that wanted to do this
tidal and wind power combination because the company
wanted to go about 20 miles offshore. Individual investors
had started the company, but they couldn't get enough
of the hardware they needed from American companies,
so they had to buy them from a Spanish company. They
needed turbine blades, which are made out of compos-
ite. Some of them are huge, 50 feet long or more. The
bigger they are, the more efficient they are. Because the
United States doesn't use a lot of wind power, American

companies aren't making equipment this size, whereas Spain has made huge strides in this industry.

Of course, at some point, somebody will realize this and think, "Wow, why don't we do this domestically?" That time is probably sooner rather than later, especially since a Spanish company has opened a plant in Fort Collins, Colorado, to build wind turbines for the U.S. market rather than transporting them from Spain. The original investors in the Rhode Island company sold the company to the Spanish turbine manufacturer, so we now have a Spanish company investing in a corporation that produces the turbines here so they can sell them in America. It's similar to the auto industry, when the Japanese car companies first started building plants in the United States.

In any case, most foreign wind power companies are very solid investments for two reasons. First, they're financed by the government in their home country, which is a major incentive from an investment point of view. If a company's government is behind it, that government is guaranteeing investments in that company. The government's guarantee is mitigating the potential loss an investor might face. After all, the government doesn't want to lose the money it invested either. So you get some safety there. The second factor that makes these solid investments is that the demand for wind power will continue to increase over time. People are going to continue to invest in wind power because it makes sense. Last but not least, most of these companies are well run.

If you're interested in investing in these well-established large companies, you need to do it via the stock exchanges in their home countries. Obviously, buying stocks in this way doesn't fit our goal of finding alternatives to the stock, bond, and mutual fund markets. But new companies are always entering the marketplace. If you believe that this is a great market that you want to be in because you can help the world make improvements in its energy consumption, look at what's available in the marketplace and keep following it to stay abreast. Again, this is part of the due diligence process. If you're interested in an emerging new market, such as wind power, you need to keep in mind that it is a new industry. Even if the industry as a whole seems to have very good potential on the upside, the newer smaller companies don't yet have a track record against which to evaluate your investment.

By the way, you shouldn't be afraid of investing offshore. Most profitable offshore companies are usually functioning well and are monitored and regulated in their home countries. Furthermore, there are ways you can make sure that these companies are doing what they say they are doing and that their finances are what they say they are. See Chapter 6 for more information on making foreign investments.

Wind power is a high-potential investing opportunity because it provides energy to various grids. Although the companies may be large, small investors can still get involved. Individuals like you can invest in energy providers that are local, and it's not difficult. Many of these energy producers find sites where a wind farm will work well, and they send potential investors a prospectus. Usually, these companies are small LLCs that provide the energy to the grid, which the grid is paying them to do. Let's say you find out about a small company that has a wind farm on a hilltop someplace. The small company owns that hilltop. You know that the company has both an agent to sell the energy produced and a buyer to buy the energy. This would probably be a good investment.

As you do your due diligence, you need to know who is supplying the wind energy. Then look at the contract to find out who they're supplying the energy to, and determine whether the buyer and seller are in fact real entities (either individuals or companies). You need to know that there really are windmills, and where they are—ideally by visiting the location yourself. Visiting the hilltop is not an absolute requirement, but doing so will give you an idea of what the wind farm really looks like. And you want to make sure that it's really there.

If you can't or don't want to visit a particular site, you can do your due diligence by researching these energy providers on the Internet or by calling the utility company and asking, "Who's supplying your energy?" The energy company usually has that information available. You need to be sure that the company you're considering investing in is supplying wind energy to an energy company such as Con Edison. Keep in mind, however, that your local energy company (again, like Con Edison) is getting energy from several providers, because (depending on state laws) energy companies are often required to buy excess energy from a local provider. Most energy providers are very small companies, at least in comparison to companies like Shell, for example. Still, those very small companies have invested hundreds of thousands of dollars in their energy operations. To assess whether you're interested in investing in these companies, evaluate how they're doing and then make your investment decision.

Many people find wind power (and the other alternative energy sources mentioned in this chapter) to be interesting investments because the supply of oil is decreasing. Investors know that individuals will be oriented more and more heavily toward alternative energies over the next three to four decades. And investors know that the demand for energy is not going away any time soon. So the investment opportunities are there. It's just a matter of doing the necessary due diligence, much as you would with any other company that you were considering investing in. You need to determine that the people you're going to be investing your money with are not bamboozling you with imaginary wind mills (as we saw in Chapter 4 with the imaginary cell phone towers in Texas) or overstated claims.

For instance, some investors were burned by investing in wind power back in the 1970s. At that time, wind tower operators believed that their technology was really sophisticated. They thought, "People are going to make so much money. We're going to generate all this power, and we're going to sell it to the power company." Well, what happened was that the equipment components they used—the turbines, the turbine blades, and the towers themselves—frequently worked poorly or broke down altogether, and the maintenance costs were enormous. These companies failed because there weren't capable suppliers in sufficient numbers to make this a mature industry. Many people lost their investments in those companies. The upshot was that in the 1970s, wind towers were a great idea whose time just hadn't come.

The Altamont Pass Wind Farm, located in Northern California about an hour east of San Francisco, was one of those projects that was built after the 1970s energy crisis. The people who were seeking money from investors *said* they had built wind farms elsewhere. They even showed pictures of wind farms that they claimed were theirs, but it turned out they weren't. These people were con artists committing fraud. We had a number of clients who had invested in Altamont Pass via their IRAs and lost all of that money. Some lost $50,000, some lost $100,000, which is a lot of money even today but was a huge amount to lose 40 years ago.

Fortunately, the wind power industry has now matured. For example, the Altamont Pass Wind Farm is still in operation but under different management. Today, it's a significant business and is growing steadily. However, I would wager that the people who lost their investments 40 years ago don't care that the industry has matured. They're probably never going to invest in that industry again. After all, once burned, twice shy.

Investing in Wave Power

Wave and tidal power is a huge energy source, though so far (like wind power), its potential is exploited mostly in Europe—several major facilities are in Scotland and Ireland. But the United States is starting to catch on to the power of waves. Back in 2003, San Francisco started to realize that its bay was a great potential source of electricity, and it decided to spend $2 million on a pilot project that would channel all that wave power. The director of the city's environmental affairs department said, "Each day, nearly 400 billion gallons of water rush through the mouth of San Francisco Bay. If harnessed, the energy from this water could be an answer to the city's power needs."[2]

Unfortunately, it turned out that the amount of power that was going in and out of the Golden Gate, where the San Francisco Bay opens onto the Pacific Ocean, wasn't sufficient to do that; it was *outside* of the Golden Gate that the power was sufficient. The other problem the developers encountered was timing: the tide goes in and out twice a

---

[2] Miguel Llanos, "San Francisco to Test Tides for Energy," MSNBC.com, May 8, 2003.

day, but consistency in electrical power delivery is needed 24 hours a day. So, even though each tidal change generated a lot of power, it happened only two times a day—not a good deal for the end users. The question then becomes, what can generate the power when the waves aren't waving, so to speak.

What they discovered in San Francisco was that the finances for this project were not economically viable to exploit the wave power in that location. Although the area that's right outside the Golden Gate is fairly significant in terms of the energy that it produces, it was expensive to build there. Over time, however, the technologies have advanced and the financial factors have changed. In 2008, San Francisco's mayor pledged that he would look into this type of power generation and reevaluate its potential.

What's really important for investors to consider is what happens when an energy source is converted to another form in order to store it and use it. Also, what happens to the excess energy produced? Can it be transferred to the grid, from where it can be sold and deployed as needed?

Right now, in the United States, more than 50 percent of the power that we consume is generated by burning coal. The United States has an interest in minimizing the amount of coal that's consumed to produce power because burning coal contributes greatly to the greenhouse gases being spewed into the atmosphere. But if we reduce the amount of coal-dependent power that we produce and use, somebody's got to produce that power some other way.

In terms of using all of the alternative fuels mentioned in this chapter, investors need to consider how energy will be produced, stored, and transported when the waves aren't waving, the wind's not blowing, and the sun's not out. Most likely, the demand for energy in any one place will have to be met with several types of energy supplies. We may never be able to fully rely on passive energy sources like solar, wind, and tidal power because people require energy throughout the day.

In 2003, in the San Francisco case, it wasn't economically viable to use tidal power to meet some of the city's energy needs. The tidal power was too far offshore to be viable. And in 2009, that's still the case. The tidal power needs to be fairly close to the shore because the farther from land, the more expensive it is to build and maintain the power generation equipment. However, that financial picture might change in the near future with advances in materials and technology.

With all alternative energy investments, investors need to investigate the proposed projects to assess whether they are truly viable. If a small energy provider tries to sell you on investing in the company by saying, "Hey, this is really going to be terrific," you need to do your homework before deciding whether to place an investment with that company. You need to ask, "Where is the power being generated? How is it better than someplace else? Can you prove to me, as the investor, that your idea has merit?"

The San Francisco project was interesting because a lot of R&D went into it; yet the upshot was that it just didn't work. That was an expensive lesson to learn for the people who invested in that project. It is a good example of why it is critical to do the necessary due diligence before you invest in anything.

CHAPTER 6

INVESTING
INTERNATIONALLY
Currency Exchange, the Forex,
Bonds, and Real Estate

There are so many good reasons why you should diversify internationally. No matter how small an investment portfolio you may have, you know the basics of diversification. Diversifying your portfolio mitigates your risk. If you have different types of investments, regardless of whether you've invested in a single industry or several, you've spread out your risk. If one company or entity that you've invested with doesn't do well, your other investments might still be okay. The whole idea of diversification in an investment portfolio is to not bear all of your risk in one place.

Typically, most American investors diversify their portfolios only among stocks, bonds, and mutual funds, and *only in the United States.* Certainly that diversification approach is better than investing 100 percent of your money in a single company (for example, Microsoft) or investing 100 percent of your money in a stock market index fund (for example, the S&P 500). But even going to the next step by investing some of your money in U.S. *equity* markets and some of your money in U.S. *bond* markets does not result in a dramatically diversified portfolio.

You can diversify into many other investment vehicles, for example, real estate. In the present downturn, people are diversifying into real estate, even as the market continues to become more difficult to navigate. These investors know that at some point the real estate market is going to expand again. And they know that when they invest in real estate, they make money when they buy, not when they sell (following the old adage, "buy low, sell high"). In addition to diversifying into real estate, many people diversify their portfolios by investing in private placements. These are not traditional investments but rather smaller investments that are not necessarily traded on the various stock exchanges. Many investors prefer making these smaller investments because they tend to be more affordable and the investors themselves can research and track them. These investors want to place their money in what they know firsthand, they want to have a more hands-on approach in managing their investments, and they want to actually visit their investments.

Diversification doesn't simply mean that you invest in different opportunities available in the stock and bond markets. If you invest solely in the stock market, when the entire market takes a nosedive, so do all your investments. Instead, diversification means that you're also investing in real estate or private placements or other alternative investments like those described throughout this book. Investing in many different types of investments is the best way to avoid getting burned.

WHY INVEST INTERNATIONALLY

Diversifying into various types of investments solely *in one country* isn't true diversification either. In addition to diversifying in your domestic market, you should *internationalize* your investments. Many people don't do this. Large companies invest internationally, of course, but most individual investors don't diversify into other countries and their marketplaces. In fact, a recent survey conducted by Schroders plc found that only 13 percent of Americans invest in international stocks.[1] As an investor, you *need* to invest internationally. Even if you're well diversified with a variety of different investments within the U.S. markets, if the U.S. economy collapses, all of those markets could be affected simultaneously and you would not be protected. You can protect your investments against that event because other economies, even today, are not having the same types of difficulties that the United States is having.

Having said that, however, with a global recession looming, diversification into other countries has its own issues, because now almost every country in the world has problems. So obviously, you need to look at those countries that aren't having problems. One of the best ways of doing that, quite simply, is to read the *Economist* magazine. The back of each issue usually includes a chart of economic indicators for overseas markets. From this chart, you can see which countries are doing well or are in a growth mode or are at least not

---

[1] According to a June 2007 telephone survey of more than 1,000 American investors over 18 years old. The survey was conducted by Schroders Investment Management North America, a unit of Schroders plc, a global asset management company with approximately $147.7 billion in assets under management as of March 31, 2009.

Exhibit 6.1

Economic Indicators for Overseas Markets

Markets	Index Mar 25th	one week	Dec 31st 2008 in local currency	Dec 31st 2008 in $ terms
			% change on	
United States (DJIA)	7,749.8	+3.5	–11.7	–11.7
United States (S&P 500)	813.9	+2.5	–9.9	–9.9
United States (NAScomp)	1,529.0	+2.5	–3.0	–3.0
Japan (Nikkei 225)	8,480.0	+6.4	–4.3	–11.2
Japan (Topix)	818.5	+7.0	–4.7	–11.6
China (SSEA)	2,405.3	+3.0	+25.8	+25.7
China (SSEB, $ terms)	151.1	+3.8	+36.4	+36.2
Britain (FTSE 100)	3,900.3	+2.5	–12.0	–10.8
Canada (S&P TSX)	8,797.4	+2.0	–2.1	–1.3
Euro area (FTSE Euro 100)	658.7	+6.2	–11.7	–14.0
Euro area (DJ STOXX 50)	2,149.2	+6.4	–12.2	–14.5
Austria (ATX)	1,700.5	+9.2	–2.9	–5.4
Belgium (Bel 20)	1,757.0	+3.4	–7.9	–10.3
France (CAC 40)	2,893.5	+4.8	–10.1	–12.4
Germany (DAX)*	4,223.3	+5.7	–12.2	–14.5
Greece (Athex Comp)	1,694.3	+7.3	–5.2	–7.6
Italy (S&P/MIB)	16,263.0	+12.4	–16.4	–18.6
Netherlands (AEX)	225.6	+7.7	–8.3	–10.7
Spain (Madrid SE)	847.8	+5.2	–13.1	–15.4
Czech Republic (PX)	807.0	+14.3	–6.0	–10.0
Denmark (OMXCB)	210.8	+1.2	–6.8	–9.3
Hungary (BUX)	11,314.5	+14.3	–7.6	–20.2
Norway (OSEAX)	276.6	+9.4	+2.4	+10.1
Poland (WIG)	25,477.2	+11.3	–6.4	–17.3
Russia (RTS, $ terms)	740.9	+13.9	+29.2	+17.3
Sweden (Aff.Gen)	196.2	+0.4	–0.5	–2.6
Switzerland (SMI)	4,970.4	+3.9	–10.2	–14.9
Turkey (ISE)	25,536.4	+8.7	–4.9	–11.4
Australia (All Ord.)	3,546.2	+4.7	–3.1	–4.1
Hong Kong (Hang Seng)	13,622.1	+3.8	–5.3	–5.3
India (BSE)	9,667.9	+7.7	+0.2	–3.8
Indonesia (JSX)	1,420.0	+7.3	+4.8	–1.0
Malaysia (KLSE)	878.8	+3.6	+0.2	–4.4
Pakistan (KSE)	6,674.2	+6.5	+13.8	+11.8
Singapore (STI)	1,691.7	+7.3	–4.0	–8.3
South Korea (KOSPI)	1,229.0	+5.0	+9.3	+1.1
Taiwan (TWI)	5,346.4	+5.9	+16.4	+12.8
Thailand (SET)	436.9	+2.5	–2.9	–4.7
Argentina (MERV)	1,132.3	+6.3	+4.9	–1.7
Brazil (BVSP)	41,799.0	+4.1	+11.3	+15.9
Chile (IGPA)	12,128.1	+1.3	+7.1	+18.9
Colombia (IGBC)	8,031.2	+1.7	+6.2	+0.5
Mexico (IPC)	20,272.8	+3.3	–9.4	–11.8
Venezuela (IBC)	42,911.4	+4.5	+22.3	+31.7
Egypt (Case 30)	4,167.2	+6.5	–9.3	–11.3
Israel (TA-100)	654.4	+7.8	+16	+5.1
Saudi Arabia (Tadawul)	4,584.2	+4.2	–4.6	–4.5

South Africa (JSE AS)	21,257.6	+9.8	−1.2	−3.2
Europe (FTSEurofirst 300)	743.9	+4.6	−10.6	−12.9
World, dev'd (MSCI)	829.4	+5.1	−9.9	−9.9
Emerging markets (MSCI)	587.4	+8.0	+3.6	+3.6
World, all (MSCI)	208.1	+5.4	−8.6	−8.6
World bonds (Citigroup)	777.4	+1.8	−4.0	−4.0
EMBI+ (JPMorgan)	400.4	+1.4	+2.3	+2.3
Hedge funds (HFRX)‡	1,030.9	+0.6	+1.0	+1.0
Volatility, US (VIX)	42.3	40.1	40.0	(levels)
CDSs Eur (iTRAXX)†	182.6	−4.5	−9.6	−12.0
CDSs, N Am (CDX)†	250.1	−6.2	+7.1	+7.1
Carbon trading (EU ETS) €	10.6	−14.2	−34.1	−35.8

*Total return index. †Credit-default swap spreads, basis points.
Sources: National statistics offices, central banks and stock exchanges;
Thomson Datastream; Reuters; W/M Reuters; JPMorgan Chase;
Bank Leumi le-Israel; CBOE; CMIE; Danske Bank; EEX; HKMA;
Markit; Standard Bank Group; UBS; Westpac. ‡Mar 24th

Source: *Economist,* March 26, 2004, print edition.

in as deep a recession as the United States. An example chart is shown in Exhibit 6.1. When you find which countries are doing less badly than others, you can then determine whether those countries have assets that you want to invest in.

How to Invest Internationally

When you spread your investment risk internationally, you're looking at really huge diversification. Most Americans tend not to diversify internationally, and of those who do, most tend to have American Depositary Receipts (also known as ADRs), which are certificates issued by U.S. banks (for example, the Bank of New York Mellon). These certificates represent a specified number of shares in a foreign stock that is traded on a U.S. stock exchange, such as the New York Stock Exchange (NYSE), the American Stock Exchange (Amex), or the NASDAQ. By buying ADRs, investors can buy shares in foreign companies and receive their dividends and interest payments in U.S. dollars. This is one way Americans invest that does have international impact. Another way some Americans invest internationally is in international mutual funds, which are composed of multiple stocks, bonds, and other financial instruments that are not only U.S. based but also international.

You can also go directly to whatever international markets interest you and invest in those particular markets. All you have to do is find and contact organizations outside the United States to be able to make those kinds of investments. You need to select a bank or financial institution in the country that you're interested in and invest through that financial institution. This has been a very common strategy among Europeans for many decades because of the proximity of all the European countries to one another.

For example, suppose you live in the United States, and you want to invest in Airbus, which is traded on the European exchanges. Airbus is a very large company (about the size of Boeing in terms of its sales and other parameters). It has 56,000 employees in more than 160 offices, with headquarters in Toulouse, France. Its parent company is EADS, which is based in Munich, Germany, with $39 billion in revenues in 2007. Germany and France have different stock markets, of course, and you can invest in Airbus on several foreign exchanges because the company does business in several countries. Or you might want to invest in some other big company such as Siemens, which also does business in many different countries and is headquartered in Germany.

In addition to huge companies, though, many small companies deal with a variety of different local investment opportunities, and it's a matter of selecting those that interest you specifically. For example, in Chapter 5, we mentioned Vestas, the Spanish company that manufactures wind turbines and blades for producing wind energy. You can invest in Vestas by going to Spain's financial markets and looking at the different stock issues that Vestas offers. As mentioned, Europeans have invested this way for decades simply because of their proximity to all the countries of Europe. They know which investing opportunities are available on the stock exchanges in neighboring countries, and they can easily visit companies in those nearby countries as well.

But you don't have to live in Europe to invest in Europe (or anywhere else). Regardless of where you live, investing in companies based in other countries isn't difficult. However, U.S. citizens cannot go directly to a non-U.S. bank to do transactions outside of the United States. If you want to use a financial institution in the country where the company that you want to invest in directly trades, you must do your own research, because the United States prohibits non-U.S. banks, foreign investment institutions, and any other foreign financial institution to advertise in the United States. This is different from almost every other country in the world, where financial institutions are *not* prohibited from advertising to potential investors. The U.S. restrictions are probably a result of a protectionist stance.

One of the things that Entrust has done is set up bank-to-bank relationships that allow our clients in the United States to connect with institutions that can provide them access to foreign markets. The process is easy, and we can do it on an accommodation basis for our clients. Otherwise, you go to your bank's representatives, tell them that you want to invest directly in a particular foreign marketplace, and ask them whether they will conduct those transactions for you. Unfortunately, however, that's not something that every bank likes to do. U.S. securities firms and banks want you to buy ADRs because they receive a cut of the action.

Because of the commission, they are more willing to help you invest via ADRs than make direct placements in foreign institutions, which doesn't bring them revenue.

For example, suppose you have an account with Charles Schwab & Co., Inc., and you tell Schwab, "I'd like to invest in Siemens, which is listed on the Frankfurt Stock Exchange and is in the DAX" (the German stock market index for blue-chip stocks). Schwab is likely to say (as would almost any other U.S. financial institution), "Well, we don't do that. Instead, what we can do for you is buy ADRs in Siemens." So Schwab connects with a financial institution in Germany, which then buys the assets on behalf of your bank, which then sells them back to you, making a percentage on the deal.

In contrast, Entrust goes *directly* to a foreign financial institution. Thus, if our clients ask us to buy Siemens stock for them, we can do it through any one of several foreign banks. That bank buys the stock that our clients want on their behalf. Note that in 2009, E*TRADE began advertising that investors could buy directly from foreign exchanges via their E*TRADE accounts, but E*TRADE was charging a considerable up-front fee to do that. Also, the program was limited to six countries at the time: Canada, France, Germany, the United Kingdom, Japan, and Hong Kong.

What to Invest in Internationally

After you overcome the logistical hurdle of finding a foreign financial institution to facilitate your investments, diversification into various countries makes a lot of sense. What you're doing is reducing your risk of being invested in only one country that might be experiencing a downturn—whether that's the United States or elsewhere. You just have to judge how well you perceive another country's economy to be performing.

Raw Materials That Power Industries around the World

One type of investment to consider is raw materials, but it's important to review their role in the global market. For example, Australia supplies raw materials to China, and for a long time, the Australian economy was doing extremely well and was expanding. Australia shipped huge amounts of coal and other energy-related products, including oil and gas, to China. China then used the raw materials and energy products to power various industries and to make consumer goods, which China then sold to the United States. So an investor might have thought, "I'm going to get to the source and invest in various industries, like iron and coal." That investor would have realized good returns.

China also invests heavily in other countries—for example, Nigeria, which is a huge oil producer. China is heavily into investing in various countries in Africa and elsewhere because they have raw materials that are fairly scarce in other parts of the world. China then uses those raw materials to manufacture products that it sells to other countries. So not only can you invest in China directly but you can also invest in the countries supplying the resources that Chinese companies use to manufacture products that it then sells to the rest of the world.

The danger in this type of diversification is that when the purchasing of goods stops or slows down, a ripple effect moves through every company and economy in that supply chain. Then, all of a sudden, you can have a serious situation as far as your investments are concerned. This sequence of events has played out in the current global downturn that we are seeing in many economies around the world. So investors have to keep an eye on their foreign placements.

Luxury Goods versus Basic Necessities

A good way to approach international investing is to invest in goods that people will *always* need to consume—that is, those things that keep civilizations going, such as consumer (as opposed to industrial) energy-related enterprises, food products, and water. People will always have to eat, and they will always have to use water. So if you look at investment opportunities that are available in a world economy (even when the world economy is slowing down), look for the products that people *need* to survive.

In a globally downward-trending economy, you might not want to be investing in high-priced vacation resorts because they're not good investments during economic downturns, recessions, and depressions. For example, for the first time in decades, the large, high-end retailers like Hermès were actually reducing their prices or keeping their prices stable for the very expensive consumer goods that they sell. Clearly, recessions in some parts of the world affect wealthy people in other parts of the world. Therefore, investments in luxury items such as vacation resorts and cruise lines or high-end retailers are not good investments at such times. When this book was being written, the high-end luxury goods sellers were reducing their prices because the dollar suddenly got stronger. That meant that the luxury goods sellers could afford to cut prices and still make a profit. In upward-trending economic times, these high-end luxury consumer goods companies earn around 46 percent in profits. In the uncertain economic climate of 2009, they were happy to earn 25 percent.

In November 2008, the *New York Times* described this trend in an article entitled "In Hard Times, No More Fancy Pants." The article cited such companies as Graff diamonds, Neiman Marcus department stores, Marine Products Corp. (which makes yachts and pleasure boats), and other luxury goods retailers and even high-end restaurants as experiencing or predicting a softening of demand for their products.

As an investor with this information, you need to decide whether you want to invest in such companies. If you believe that very wealthy people are going to continue to spend money on high-end luxury goods, those companies might be good investments. But you also need to consider how many wealthy people there are. Again, in tougher economic times, it's probably safer to invest in companies that satisfy a worldwide demand for necessities, not luxury goods.

Real Estate

Global real estate is also a really good opportunity, but you need to take the long view, especially during a recession or a depression (although we advocate the long view even in a strong economy). By the long view, we mean about 20 years.

If you are interested in offshore real estate, you can easily begin your research on the Internet. There are some good Web sites out there that describe what the individual rules are for most countries on the planet. Those sources even give you guidance on how to actually make the transaction. Exhibit 6.2 lists a few useful Web sites.

As we've emphasized throughout this book, doing due diligence before you invest in anything is absolutely critical. When you're considering investing in real estate in a foreign country here are the basics of what you need to do. First, you should visit the country you're considering

Exhibit 6.2

Web Sites That Offer Information on Buying Real Estate in Other Countries

- www.globalpropertyguide.com. This Web site is a good source for researching different countries. It provides information on price history, taxes, landlord-tenant laws, inheritance laws, and so on.
- www.fiabci.com. The International Real Estate Federation (FIABCI), headquartered in Paris, promotes the real estate profession. Its members are from 60 countries, drawing on 100 national real estate associations representing 1.5 million professionals, including agents, lawyers, appraisers, and property managers.
- www.justlanded.com. This Web site provides information in different languages on how to obtain travel visas; how to find jobs, housing, and work permits; and how to find properties for sale or rent. In its country guides, it posts lists of resources for a variety of countries.
- www.transparency.org. Transparency International, headquartered in Berlin, is a politically nonpartisan organization that monitors all types of corruption, including politics, public contracting, land development, and the private sector. This site can help you learn about possible construction and land development scams—and protect yourself!
- www.icrea.org. The International Consortium of Real Estate Associations (ICREA) sets standards for international real estate practices and facilitates worldwide real estate transactions. Its Web site has links to resources and information for a variety of countries.
- www.rics.org. The Royal Institute of Chartered Surveyors (RICS), based in Coventry, England, promotes global

standards for professionals involved in land, property, construction, and environmental issues. This Web site contains links to members in different countries.

• www.cepi.be. The European Council of Real Estate Professions (CEPI) is based in Belgium. This organization represents 200,000 European Union real estate professionals. The council's Web site provides links to property managers and property agents.

Source: Reprinted from Hubert Bromma, *How to Invest in Offshore Real Estate and Pay Little or No Taxes*, McGraw-Hill, 2008, pp. 201–202.

investing in. This sounds like a no-brainer ("Who would buy real estate in a county they've never been to?"), but we've heard of and met investors who have done exactly that.

For example, Costa Rica has been a destination for many American investors for at least 20 years. Once known as the "Switzerland of the Americas," many U.S. sales agents went there to pick up properties and resell them to investors that they cultivated in the United States. An investor would send money to an agent, who would give the investor details and pictures of the investment property and would then purchase the property on the investor's behalf. Then the hard part came: renting the property and gathering the income, and dealing with tax matters, repairs, and vacancies. In more than one case, the property that was bought had significant problems, and the investor's cash flow evaporated. The sales agent then "got a new cell phone." More than once. When the investors finally realized they had to personally visit their property to see what was happening, they often found that their tenants were not the people the investors thought they were. This is why it is important to have an experienced, capable, and trustworthy property manager and to see firsthand what your investment actually consists of.

Also, do you speak the language? This is just 1 of about 50 points that we think are critical to consider before you purchase property in another country. And even if you speak the language or find someone local who speaks *your* language, you should hire local attorneys who know their country's real estate laws and who can advise you on the legality of the investments you're interested in making.

But unfortunately, just because someone speaks your language doesn't make that person trustworthy. We know of one German investor who wanted to buy property for re-tirement in Spain. He found a German contractor working in Spain. Because they spoke the same language and be-cause the contractor was German, the investor felt he could trust him. But that contractor took the investor's €250,000 and left him high and dry, with no investment property and no home to move to when he retired. What this German investor should have done was retain a Spanish attorney who could have told him that construction corruption is rife in Spain. If he had checked out www.transparency. org, one of the Web sites listed in Exhibit 6.2, he would have found that out—so you can protect yourself and your money.

So you need to do your own research. Just because someone speaks what seems like flawless English (or whatever your native language is), that doesn't mean a darn thing because that person might not know anything about the investment you're interested in. Moreover, when you talk to locals in a country that you're interested to invest in, they obviously don't know what you know about their country—or what you *don't* know about their country. They can't advise you about real estate or any other alternative investing. They'll be happy to take your money, but that's not the way to invest safely. You need to know the rules yourself. The German investor admitted after he got burned on his property purchase in Spain, "Knowing Spanish and a little bit about Spain's real estate law would have helped a lot." That's an understatement.

For more in-depth information about investing in offshore real estate, consult an earlier book that Hugh wrote, *How to Invest in Offshore Real Estate and Pay Little or No Taxes* (McGraw-Hill, 2008).

TAKING THE LONG VIEW WHEN INVESTING INTERNATIONALLY

When you take the long view in investing, and you have the cash to invest and the interest to educate yourself, you can take advantage of what you have the foresight to see as a good investment for your portfolio. For example, 20 years from now, the cost of producing oil is going to increase, which will in turn increase the price that we see at the gas pump. Right now, the fluctuations we're seeing are anomalies. In only one year, the price went up to over $4 a gallon during the summer of 2008 and came down to $2 a gallon in early 2009. Obviously, these dramatic price changes had nothing to do with supply and demand. Instead, they were a result of markets being affected by individuals who are true capitalists.

The idea here is to invest in scarce goods that are and will be required for production of some necessity—for example, energy. You might also consider investing in replacement goods—consumers can use wind-generated power instead of oil-generated power. Some replacement goods are so scarce today that they're ridiculously expensive, but in the future, they will become less expensive. This is why we devoted Chapter 5 to solar, wind, and wave power. They already command a larger part of the energy used by individuals worldwide. This is especially true in Europe. In 2009, in Denmark, 20 percent of the power used was from wind power, and in Germany, it was 9 percent. But in the United States, only 1 percent of the power used was from wind power. So Americans are lagging far behind Europe.

Such imbalances open up investing opportunities for U.S. investors who are interested in researching what will be the replacements for petroleum products and eventually for natural gas. Currently, 75 percent of the gas and oil that Americans use is produced domestically in the United States. But that's going to change, and we're going to have to start making trade-offs, as the Europeans have. Germany and Denmark don't have a lot of petroleum reserves, and their natural gas supplies come from eastern Europe—principally, from Russia. So if you're interested in diversifying your investments internationally, try to think about what the world might look like in 20 years, and ask yourself: "What will our energy requirements be? How much will the population expand? Where are those products going to be manufactured or produced?" After you've come up with some possible answers and scenarios, you can invest accordingly—either in large companies that are already listed on international stock markets or in smaller, innovative start-ups (we'll describe more about how to do that, domestically or internationally, in Chapter 8).

We had a client in Hawaii who decided during the summer of 2008 that she wanted to actively diversify outside of her U.S. portfolio. She was interested in investing specifically in emerging markets in central Europe. She decided her investment portfolio should consist of foreign equities and real property. She contacted us and said, "I want to buy into oil and natural gas ventures in eastern Europe and pipelines that carry the gas to western Europe from eastern Europe and Russia."

We don't know how she chose oil and natural gas ventures— we're not permitted to ask those questions. By the time she approached us with her plan, she had already decided where she wanted to invest. She was a member of the Sovereign Society, which is a libertarian group of individuals who are interested in investing offshore. Through her association with the society and other similar sources, she had educated herself about this type of investment. She came to us with her investing plan and asked us how to do it. We facilitated the logistics by making the relevant foreign financial institutions available to her. Not many companies have the types of contacts we have, which is why she came to us. She had heard that we have a contact bank in Europe through which she could make the types of investments that she was interested in.

She invested via her regular portfolio and her IRA into a separate account with the financial institution in Europe. She opened an account with our Hawaii office, and then she directed us to open an account on her behalf with the bank in Europe. She then instructed the European bank as to what she wanted to purchase for her portfolio. After the purchase had been made, we put it into her IRA portfolio, where we would continue to keep the records for it. This was a substantial account. In her IRA portfolio alone, she had $2 million, so obviously, with a couple million dollars, she could diversify pretty well.

How Much Money Do You Need to Invest Internationally?

The example of our Hawaiian client brings up an important point: You can't really diversify globally with $50,000 because you would have to spread that total too thinly. In fact, the Europeans say you need half a million bucks, minimum.

There are companies that will take $100,000; still, the level of diversification you'll achieve is very, very small. At that amount, your investment will tend to be a managed account, where the European investment company or bank manages your account as part of a large pool of investments that it makes. In other words, the company combines your $100,000 with other people's $100,000 investments so that it can actually make some investments that are intelligent. And when you look at the types of investments that these companies make, $100,000 is not a lot of money.

For those investors who have only $10,000 to invest, this type of international investing just isn't feasible. With this amount, if you're interested in diversifying globally, you might as well buy a global mutual fund, which is still a good idea. After all, if you want to start diversifying your investments beyond your local economy, you have to put your money somewhere. So you should look, for example, at an international index fund and consider the following factors:

- The quality of the fund
- What the fund manager is doing with it

- Whether the fund manager is investing in programs that you believe in
- Whether the fund manager's investments are where you want to diversify your investments over the next 10 or 20 years

These are the same factors you would consider for any mutual fund. And, just as with your domestic mutual funds, you need to review your investments every year and see if you need or want to adjust anything, assess their performance, and determine whether the intelligence that you've gathered personally compares with what the mutual fund company is doing with your investment.

BEING PATIENT WHEN INVESTING INTERNATIONALLY

The example of our client in Hawaii also brings up another important point: You can't make this type of investment immediately, like you can when you buy stocks or invest in mutual funds via a broker. It took our client about two months from the time she decided where she wanted to invest and the time that her transaction was completed. She also did a lot of active research and due diligence, which is critically important in this type of transaction.

In that particular example, she wanted to invest in emerging markets. She surveyed all the companies that dealt with eastern European goods and services, and she researched via the Internet and via an international investment seminar. She found out about a natural gas pipeline that was being built in ex-Soviet Georgia, and she contacted the leaders of that company. She knew that building a pipeline there was a viable alternative energy source because, as a result, the Russians wouldn't be able to dominate the natural gas supply coming out of eastern Europe—that is, out of Kazakhstan, Uzbekistan, and other countries. She also knew that the pipeline was being built by an Austrian company. She even traveled to Vienna (which is the type of due diligence we've been recommending throughout this book) to visit the company. And she selected an Austrian financial institution to make her investments.

She completed her investment within two months, which isn't a lot of time in the scheme of things. Nevertheless, many investors are impatient and think that is a lot of time. They want immediate gratification, and their attitude is, "I want to do this *now*." But it's best to take whatever time is necessary to make these types of decisions. And again, you should revisit your investment decisions regularly and keep your finger on the pulse of what's going on in the country in which you're investing.

Foreign Bonds

Another way to invest internationally is to buy foreign bonds, which are debt instruments. Bonds are pretty much the same all over the world.

For instance, we've bought Australian bonds, and we're getting 9½ percent interest on them, which is a good rate of return. The only reason we chose to invest in them is because they were doing well at the time. The Australian market's interest rates have gone down considerably, but the rate of return on our bonds stays the same.

When this book was being written, the Australian dollar had tanked by 40 percent relative to the U.S. dollar.

But we invest for the long term, and our expectation is that the Australian dollar will return to the same levels it was at when we bought the bonds in July 2008. So on a long-term basis, we're not going to lose. That will be true even if it takes many years for the Australian dollar to rebound. Relative to the U.S. dollar, it might take three years to return to even reach par with what we've invested. But after that, we've got another 15 years at 9½ percent, so we're not repatriating that money necessarily to the United States. Instead, we can repatriate that into Australian dollars, which gets into how currency exchange works, so let's take a look at that.

MAKING MONEY FROM CURRENCY EXCHANGES

Suppose you've done all your research, and you've decided which countries you want to invest in to diversify your portfolio internationally. The next factor you need to consider is currency, because the values of currencies fluctuate. Specifically, you should consider the following:

- What are the currencies you're going to be dealing in?
- What is the state of the economy in those countries, relative to their currencies?

Investing using foreign currencies isn't actually that difficult, although a lot of people think it is. What we're describing in this section is buying something (from stock in a company to foreign bonds to real estate in other countries) in U.S. dollars, which are then converted to another currency. In such situations, you don't necessarily want to repatriate the return on your investment in that foreign currency back into U.S. dollars, because you might not make as much money on your investment.

In the example we mentioned earlier regarding our buying Australian bonds, we might decide to put the money we make on that investment into another currency that is more favorable to the Australian dollar relative to the U.S. dollar. In that case, we would be dealing with multiple currencies. In other words, you wouldn't automatically say, "When my investment matures, I'll bring the profit back to the United States." You would do that only if the relative exchange rate were in your favor.

There are no restrictions on currency exchange. When you invest through an international bank, you can choose your currency, which is a nice benefit. But more important than (or at least as important as) choosing the currency that you want to be in is choosing the type of investment. You're going to want to invest in something in a country where the currency is favorable to you.

When you are making investments in currency that fluctuates, the value of what you're investing in is changeable relative to the currency. So if you're in a currency that's suddenly going upside down, you have to be aware that you have a lot of risk. For example, if you bought an Australian CD in 2008 and you were getting a 9 percent return and it was at par with the U.S. dollar, you were getting 9 percent not only in Australian dollars but also in U.S. dollars. And you would have actually done better in the United States because the U.S. dollar was down so much in comparison to the Australian dollar. In fact, in that example, you might have made 30 percent in U.S. dollars. If you did the converse, you would lose money, because you would lose money on the currency part of the investment.

For example, I know someone (let's call her Bernadette) who purchased property in New Zealand and made a good return on it. Bernadette bought six single-family dwellings, and she worked with a local property manager to rent them out. All of the units generated a positive cash flow. Being a landlord in New Zealand is not as off-putting as it might be in other parts of the world because the laws for rentals in New Zealand are strict. The property owner receives weekly payments (instead of monthly) that are automatically debited from a tenant's account (so the owner doesn't have to rely on the tenant sending a check). If a tenant is even just one week behind in paying rent, technically, the property owner can evict that tenant.

Bernadette found these New Zealand opportunities and learned the local real estate laws just by being a world traveler. She's very smart, and she's always on the lookout for a good investment opportunity. She's made a lot of investments in the United States. The New Zealand opportunity arose when the New Zealand dollar was doing well, so she realized that she could get a really good rate of return and that it was a lot cheaper to buy a rental property in New Zealand than in the United States. She paid about $60,000 for each property. They were nice properties. We have visited them, and we have even stayed in one of them.

So Bernadette had six positive-cash-flow properties, which meant that she was able to easily manage the debt she took on to buy them. The point here is that she took her returns on these investment properties in New Zealand dollars, and she *kept* that money in New Zealand dollars. She didn't repatriate that money into U.S. dollars because the exchange rate would have worked against her. As long as she didn't need the money in the United States, she kept the income in New Zealand and consumed those New Zealand dollars in the local economy when she visited, which was more favorable to her.

She could also have used the cash returns to invest in other countries in denominations that she chose. For example, suppose Bernadette decided she wanted to buy property in South Africa because the rand was not doing well against the New Zealand dollar. In that case, she could have gotten a real bargain in South Africa and bought property there. We know people who have done exactly that. And Bernadette could have done the same thing as she did in New Zealand, but this time, she could invest her New Zealand dollars and keep her profits in South African rands.

In other words, don't automatically bring back to your local market the money you make in your foreign investments if your local currency isn't strong. When you make money in foreign countries, consider the currency exchange rates when deciding where you're going to invest your earnings and where you're going to hold them.

Fortunately, when you're investing on a world currency stage, you don't have to have millions. The amount you need depends on what you invest in. Real estate can be a very good play, but you have to have the ability to manage that investment from afar or be there periodically the way Bernadette did to look at her properties and make sure everything was going well. You need to understand how world monetary systems work and how money moves from one country to another. You also need to know the local laws regarding how to invest in real estate in a particular country. This is not for the unwary, and it's not the type of investment for which you can say to yourself, "Oh, I'm going to New Zealand on vacation, and maybe I'll buy some property while I'm there."

With any foreign investment that you're considering, you need to do your due diligence on the local economy you're contemplating. Here's an example of a place that was not a smart investment. A few years ago, a lot of European investors visited the Black Sea in Bulgaria and thought, "Oh, wow, the Black Sea is such a beautiful place. We should invest there." So Bulgarian companies started building thousands and thousands of properties, and many people began investing on construction in Bulgaria. They thought it was a great investment because the Black Sea is such a nice place. Unfortunately, not that many people want to travel to Bulgaria. There was an abundance of construction projects in Bulgaria, but they were not being sold or rented.

So those investors made unintelligent decisions because they didn't look at the opportunity with common sense or logic. After all, when you build hundreds of thousands of units, people have to go there to use them, and why would they go there, especially if there's no economy, it isn't a huge vacation spot, and it's too far away. For most Europeans, Bulgaria is farther away than Spain, so why would they go to Bulgaria? The end result was that there were so many units on the Black Sea that were not being used by anyone that they became available for bargain-basement prices. But no one wanted to invest in those properties even at those low prices!

So those are the types of factors related to the local economy that you need to stir into your investing decisions. Does the opportunity make sense? You need to step away from the transaction and ask yourself, "Is there an economy that supports this tourism? Are there people who will support the economy, or not?"

Although the Black Sea real estate deals were not successful investments, there are successful investing stories, like the example we describe in Chapter 9. In that situation, some American physicians invested years ago in Mexico, but their investments languished until years later when the local infrastructure was finally developed. The refurbished highway system made travel to those investment locations much more accessible and easy. So you have to consider that maybe people are not vacationing in Bulgaria now, but the world is always looking for the next hot spot, and maybe in 15 years, Bulgaria will be it. None of us has a crystal ball, however, so this is the type of investment opportunity for which you have to gather a huge amount of information to try to determine whether the place will ever attract people sufficiently for you to make a good return on your investment. Bulgaria is in the sphere of the European community, but it's also one of the most corrupt places in the world. The individual who invests in Bulgaria has to take that into consideration as well.

If you invest in a country with a stable government and a stable economy, you tend to have less risk than if you invest in a less stable country such as Nigeria. Even though Nigeria has enormous quantities of oil, its government is unstable, and rebel factions are operating everywhere. We've advocated taking the long view, but in the case of Nigeria, the long view is probably 100 years, so that's obviously not a feasible time horizon for investing. Unfortunately, Africa is full of kleptocracies, and Nigeria is one of the best known.

Similarly, Venezuela is another country that's intriguing from an investing point of view but very risky. Many people believe it's going to be a "socialist paradise," but that system hasn't worked out too well in the past in other countries. And is socialism a situation that's going to work out favorably for investors? Right now, not many people are investing in Venezuela. The only investors are large oil conglomerates, and they're either making deals or withdrawing from Venezuela altogether because of the risks.

THE BIG QUESTIONS TO CONSIDER BEFORE INVESTING INTERNATIONALLY

When investing internationally, consider these key points. We call these "the big questions," although there are other factors that are specific to the type of international investment that you're considering that you should also take into account.

1. Are there internal issues—such as civil unrest, a repressive government, a history of military intervention in political matters, an upsurge in religious fundamentalism, racial hostilities, pervasive distrust of foreigners—that might make the country unstable in your lifetime or in the lifetime of those whom you hope to someday benefit from your investments?

2. Are there corruption issues—national or regional government corruption or failure to prosecute those engaged in nefarious business dealings? Did you consult Transparency International's corruption perception index (www.transparency.org) to get up-to-date information?

3. Are there external issues—such as border problems with neighboring countries, influxes of immigrants or refugees, overt or covert threats of terrorism—that might make the country unstable?

4. Are there foreseeable ecological concerns— pollution, deforestation, overfarming, water or

food shortages, effects of global warming, particularly on coastal areas—that might make the country's economic future less desirable?

5. Are there societal and cultural changes— religious or tribal strife, large immigrant populations, increasing disparity between rich and poor, underfunded or collapsing educational systems—that might make the stability of the country's overall future less predictable?[2]

If you answered yes to any of the above, you should do more research on the particular type of investment that you're considering making in that country.

---

[2] Hubert Bromma, *How to Invest in Offshore Real Estate and Pay Little or No Taxes*, McGraw-Hill, New York, 2008, pp. 91–92.

CHAPTER

7

INVESTING IN REAL ESTATE IN TODAY'S ECONOMY
Watch Out!

This chapter focuses primarily on investing in residential properties. The only type of commercial real estate we cover here is buying storage units for rental income. Of course, you can buy other commercial property for investment purposes, such as office buildings, shopping malls, and strip centers, but we're just not addressing it. The residential real estate market at the time we're writing this book is generally dismal for sellers, but that means it's a buyer's—and an investor's—market.

You can invest in residential property in various ways—rental properties, mobile homes, short sales, deeds in lieu of foreclosure, and properties that are already in foreclosure. You might be interested in buying tax liens or tax deeds. You can buy properties on a lease option basis, out of bankruptcy, at auctions, or out of probate. Or you might be interested in buying storage units or entire storage facilities as an alternative to traditional residential real estate.

In terms of the financing arrangements, there are only a few ways to buy homes. One is to pay cash, but few of us have a few hundred thousand or a million dollars just lying around until we find an investment that we like. The other way, and the usual way of investing in real estate, is to get a loan from a bank or a private lender. You might also get the seller to take monthly payments in the terms of the sale, which is called seller financing. If there's an existing loan, you might be able to negotiate with the bank to take over the payments.

Looking for Bargains in a Depressed Real Estate Market

Obviously, the real estate market today is in the dumps. In late 2008, Moody's predicted that the following areas would have the most significant drop in real estate in 2009 (and probably for the next few years): Atlanta, Boston, Chicago, Houston, Los Angeles, Miami, New York, Philadelphia, and Washington, D.C. To add to that bleak forecast, here are a few other statistics:

- According to the U.S. Census Bureau, in 2008, 18.6 million homes in the United States were sitting vacant, which is more than at any other time since the Census Bureau started tracking this in the 1960s.
- At the start of 2009, 2.8 percent of U.S. mortgage loans were at least three months in arrears, which was up from 1.4 percent in 2008—in other words, twice as many. And this increase is supposed to

continue through most of 2009. For example, the *News-Press* in Fort Myers, Florida, reported that one in seven homeowners were behind in their payments as of March 2009.

- If what we have is a recession that lasts for more than three-quarters of a year, economists have predicted that the number of foreclosures will go much higher, as much as 20 percent more than what's already anticipated, according to the National Association of Realtors. Damage will likely hit areas that have so far escaped many problems, including New York City.

This forecast doesn't mean that *all* real estate is declining in value—that's absolutely not the case. Optimists like Lawrence Yun, chief economist of the National Association of Realtors, anticipate prices actually going up from the middle to the end of 2009. In fact, March 2009 had a tiny rise in residential real estate, $^1/_{10}$ of 1 percent according to the *MarketWatch* newsletter.

Can you determine your investing strategy by listening to all these people? Honestly, we think you can't. We think you need to develop your own investing plan, stay focused, and invest accordingly. And your plan depends on who you are and what you're trying to accomplish.

For example, if you're thinking about selling a property to buy something else, our suggestion is to wait until 2010. Most economists are predicting that real estate in 2010 should be a bit stronger because inventory will decrease and, therefore, supply and demand will balance again. Because builders aren't building, there won't be a glut of new properties. People still need a place to live, and even the rental market will increase. On the other hand, if you're interested in buying real estate for investment purposes (or even just to live in), you want to buy below the market. Here are a few Web sites to research how affordable houses are in the market you're trying to go after:

- *www.nahb.org/hoi.* The Web site of the National Association of Home Builders ranks U.S. cities by affordability and how much prices went up or down. For example, suppose you're an investor in St. Louis, Missouri. You can find out what happened to your local real estate market in 2008, which can help you base your own projections and develop your financial picture in terms of whether you want to buy.

- *www.realtytrac.com.* This site tracks foreclosures in any area of the country. It's an excellent site to utilize if your strategy is buying homes that are priced under market.

- *www.cnnmoney.com/realestate.* This is a good place to check interest rates. If you're getting conventional financing, you can find out where you are in the current market. The subprime mess has meant that banks now have cash to lend out, but few people are taking advantage of the loan availability, so mortgage rates are starting to fall again. In fact, when we first started writing this book, mortgage rates were at 6.2 percent for a 30-year, fixed-interest loan. But by early 2009, the rates had dropped to 4.875 percent, which is incredibly low. We haven't seen rates that low in years.

- *www.rentometer.com.* If you're selling or buying a property, you can find out what the mortgage payment would be. Also, if you're trying to determine a price for a rental property, this site lists the fair market rents for where your property is located. If you're in an area where there aren't many rentals available, the rentometer can give you an idea based on square footage or the number of bedrooms.

- *www.esri.com/data.* This site provides community data by Zip code. If you're interested in a particular neighborhood, you can find the median price of homes in that neighborhood as well as the median income of people who would be trying to buy or rent in that area.
- *www.zillow.com.* This site also provides community data by Zip code. You can check houses that are for sale and foreclosures in a particular Zip code.

These are just a few sites that you can take advantage of if you're an investor who's interested in buying real estate. These Web sites provide objective information, and in today's market, such information is truly critical.

HOW TO FIND GREAT DEALS ON REAL ESTATE INVESTMENTS

When the real estate market is down, that's obviously a buyer's market—which is exactly the market investors should be looking for. It's also a good time to buy real estate if you're interested in renting it out, which is what we, as investors, are personally most interested in. However, just because that's *our* strategy doesn't mean that strategy is right for you. For example, many investors in the past were interested only in buying property, holding it for a year and a day—so that they could get the tax benefit—and then turning around and selling it.

If you're interested in buying now, absolutely phenomenal deals are out there. You just have to know how to take advantage of them. For example, you can buy now and hold until 2010 (or later) because, as mentioned, everything we're hearing is predicting that in 2010 the real estate market will begin to see an improvement in terms of higher prices and more sales. So until then, we have a buying opportunity, whether you decide to buy property at a low price and wait (with the property empty or you living in it) until you can sell it for a higher price or use it as a rental while waiting for a higher price or holding it for the long term. Whatever your objectives, consider buying right now like mad and keeping those properties, perhaps as straight rentals, for however long your investing strategy is. If you are considering buying property, here are some suggestions on finding good deals.

Look for Property That Has Been on the Market for a While

In most areas of the country, now is a great time to look at properties because homes have been sitting on the market for six months or more. Looking in market areas that have become somewhat stagnant has two benefits:

1. You might be able to get some seller financing out of the deal if there's any equity in the property.
2. You might be able to drive a relatively hard bargain. Many real estate agents have noticed that for properties that have been on the market six months or longer, the average first offer price from buyers in the current market is 15 percent below the seller's asking price. Always remember something very

important: The seller's asking price is the seller's first offer. In this market, a seller is just praying that *somebody* will buy. In the current real estate market, Barry Miller, a buyer's agent in Denver, suggests that your first offer should be somewhere around 15 percent below the seller's asking price. (And that advice applies nationwide, not just in Denver!) You may end up having to pay more, but that's a good starting point for your negotiations.

Improve Your Credit Score So You Can Buy Property More Easily

You must have a good credit score—and if you don't, try to improve it. Lenders have been tightening their belts and being more restrictive about to whom they're willing to lend money. More than ever, a low credit score could cost you, even to the point of losing out on a great investment opportunity. To get traditional financing for a property, you must have a credit score of 680 or higher. To get the best rate on a mortgage, you need a score in the range of 780 to 820. A perfect score is 850, and that is an A++ credit rating. If your credit score is below 680, you're going to pay a higher interest rate on your mortgage, if you can get one.

If you can boost your credit score, for example, from 660 to 740, you can lower your mortgage rate by a quarter of a point or more. Lenders are also getting very strict. No-document loans—loans not backed up by income verification documents—are out of the question if you decide to try bank financing, no matter what your credit score is.

If your credit score is low, one good way to improve it is to pay down your credit card debt. However, do *not* close any credit cards. We have found that closing credit card accounts actually *lowers* your credit score, and the Mortgage Brokers Association supports this finding. If you're not using the credit card, that's fine, but leave the account open. Look at your payment history. Be sure that you're making your payments on time, month after month, because that is what the credit bureau reporting agencies look for when adjusting a credit score.

If you have a high credit score, you can get a favorable interest rate on your mortgage, which, of course, will help you get a better deal, and that will give you more leeway in terms of the price point of properties you can buy.

Buyer Beware: New Legislation Is Impacting Real Estate Investors

Up until 2008 or so, not many people were familiar with some of the terminology that has (unfortunately) become all too commonplace since the decline in the real estate market. We're referring here to properties that are either *short sales* or in one of the various stages of foreclosure. These are strategies that investors, as well as homeowners, use to buy property. But, as we've emphasized so many times throughout this book, you need to *do your due diligence* (look what happened to those who invested with Bernie Madoff!) before you decide to operate in any of these different types of markets.

As we are writing this book, we are seeing more and more legislative changes every day, and some of these strategies are actually against the law in certain states. For example, Colorado is currently evaluating a law that would make it illegal for people to buy foreclosures as investments. The legislature is taking this action because they are concerned that investors will rip off the people living in the house who couldn't make their mortgage payments and had to sell. Before the subprime mortgage crisis caused the recent increase in the number of foreclosures, you could buy a foreclosure for pennies on the dollar in Colorado. Now, however, this proposed law would limit how much of a deal an investor can get.

We're going to see more and more such legislation, so to protect yourself, check the current laws before you buy. Some things may be grandfathered into these new laws to allow for investors who bought foreclosed properties a long time ago. You should also check if there are landlord or tenant law changes in your specific real estate market, because not all real estate markets are identical. To find that information, go to your local state government's Web site, look for the department of real estate, and search for legislative changes or landlord-tenant changes.

As members of the National Real Estate Investors Association, we see changes constantly on an unbelievable array of issues. Here are just a few examples:

- Some states have laws requiring tenants to request storage permits under a landlord agreement, and the landlords can charge more for this type of agreement.
- California has laws pending about smoking in rental units.
- New York passed a law in 2007 called the Granny Law that is intended to curb predatory attacks by those who target the elderly in rental units and that increases the liability of landlords for their tenants' safety.
- Pennsylvania is making changes that require multifamily rental units (specifically, properties that have more than four units) to be inspected on a more regular basis. Inspections are to check the units

for lead, mold, and other environmental issues. If you're investing in this type of property, consider the costs of these additional inspections.

- Rhode Island laws require that rental units must be certified that they are free from lead, which again may increase your costs as an investor-landlord.
- Massachusetts has a new law to protect renters' rights. If a renter files for bankruptcy, that person's tenancy is still protected under the lease, no matter what the lease says.
- Milwaukee is considering charging a tax to landlords who own rental property. The city is taking this step because, as the economy worsens, it needs additional sources of revenue.

These laws can increase your costs, which reduces the profitability of your real estate investments. So, again, *do your due diligence* through the department of real estate in your state. If you're still uncertain, you can check out your state's real estate laws at your local government's courthouse, either in the land office or the law library.

In addition to new laws that might affect your property's profitability, there are other factors that you need to be aware of. For example, one fairly new problem relates to illicit drugs, especially crystal methamphetamine (meth). If one of your tenants is cooking meth in your rental property, it is a nightmare to remediate the damage done because there are no guarantees that the meth did not seep into the foundation, and you might never get rid of it. Screening tenants is vital to your success as a landlord. The good news is that there are many laws that protect the landlord—that is, *you*, if you've invested in a property to rent it out—so the laws are not necessarily only in favor of tenants. Still, before you buy anything—whether you're going to hold a property for a year or forever—you need to know the laws in your state as they apply to you (as an investor) and as they apply to landlords in general.

BUYING SHORT SALES

Investing in short sales is one way investors can buy property to take advantage of the current buyer's market. Of course, real estate is an ever-changing credit and lending market, so anything can change tomorrow.

Because we're real estate investors, we are often asked, "Which is better: a foreclosure or a short sale?" From the seller's standpoint, neither is desirable, but the major difference is how each affects the seller's credit. For the seller, a foreclosure is worse than a short sale. But for the purposes of this book, we're looking at the pros and cons from the buyer's point of view—especially when the buyers are investors.

If a borrower lets a home go into foreclosure, the borrower can live in the property for several months after the foreclosure until actually evicted. I know of one case in which the property owner had been foreclosed on, but the bank has not been able to sell the property, so the owner is living in it mortgage free. The consensus from real estate agents in the area was that it is better to leave the foreclosed party in the property than incur vandalism or other expenses that the bank would be responsible for. When you buy a property out of foreclosure, keep in mind that patience is required because the people who have lost their home will have a hard time leaving.

Short sales are a bit different from foreclosures. In real estate, short sale refers to a situation in which borrowers sell their property for less than the amount they owe on the mortgage—in other words, the proceeds fall short of the debt. When a borrower sells property via a short sale and lists the property with a real estate agent to find buyers or investors, the real estate agent needs to disclose that the property is being sold as a short sale.

The seller expects to receive a lowball offer from buyers, and if the seller works with investors to speed up the sale of the property, the seller will likely receive a *really* lowball offer. Also, the lender who holds the mortgage usually will not tell the seller what price it might accept until after an offer comes in. This is very important because, although buying short sales sounds easy, no one knows for sure what the lender is willing to take until the seller receives a written offer from a buyer. The lender has the right to respond to the interested buyer by saying, "Your offer isn't enough money, so we're not willing to make this deal." When you make an offer, you're simply trying to get the lender to *begin* negotiating. In the past, a seller needed to be behind on the mortgage payments to negotiate a short sale. In contrast, today most lenders will consider a short sale on most loans.

In many cases, the overall condition of the home determines whether the lender agrees to accept a short sale. If the home is in good condition, the lender is not going to short too much. Also, if the seller has a lot of cash assets, a higher income, or if the buyer is a real estate investor, the bank might be less inclined to negotiate with the potential buyer. Sometimes banks are more open to negotiate on a short sale with a potential owner-occupant—somebody who is actually going to live in the house—than with an investor. That's another important distinction that most investors don't understand when they're considering buying short sales: The bank might not want to sell to you!

If you want to purchase a short sale, you must first make an offer, but not to the seller. Instead, you must contact the lender or put an offer in writing to the lender. Prior to your letter, the seller should send a hardship letter (the sadder, the better for both parties) that states that he just can't afford to make the payments anymore and that you are coming in to save the day. In addition, the seller should submit a letter of authorization to the lender. This letter is necessary because lenders typically won't disclose any personal information without written authorization to do so. You'll receive better cooperation from the lender if the seller gives the lender permission to talk with interested parties about the deal. The letter to the lender should simply say that the seller is happy with this deal and that the lender should cooperate with you because you're interested in buying the property. You, as the investor, need to have proof of your incoming assets and copies of your bank statements (just as you would when buying any real estate). In addition, it's very helpful to have a comparative market analysis that shows how the real estate market in the area in which you're buying has declined in value, which gives further incentive to the lender to welcome your offer.

Even if you're working with a real estate agent, you need to do your due diligence (as we keep emphasizing!) to determine whether the property has any environmental hazards or structural problems. If a home inspection has already been done, you might want to submit that to the lender so that they can see that a short sale would be beneficial to get this property off their books. Keep in mind that even if you provide all this information, the lender can still say no to the deal that you're offering. But if you can get the lender to agree to your offer, a short sale can be a very good investment because you're buying smart.

Buying Deeds in Lieu of Foreclosure

It's often easier to buy a deed in lieu of foreclosure than it is to buy a property that's already in foreclosure because it's a better way for homeowners to get out from under debt. Selling property as a deed in lieu of foreclosure doesn't ruin the seller's credit as much as going into foreclosure. In some respects, buying a deed in lieu of foreclosure is almost the same as buying a short sale because the seller is saying to prospective buyers: "I can't afford the property, so here, please take it off my hands."

Lisa has invested in several deeds in lieu of foreclosure. For example, she bought a property in North Carolina from a man named Randy, who had a first mortgage with Wachovia Bank and a second mortgage with a finance company. Lisa first got involved when Randy was behind in his payments for his second mortgage. She negotiated with the second mortgage holder and bought the loan, which meant that Lisa made the mortgage payments on the second mortgage. Then Lisa was notified that Randy was also behind on his first mortgage and on the verge of losing the property, so she wrote him a letter that basically said, "I see that you're behind on your payments. Would you be willing to talk about my buying the property from you?" Randy agreed to meet with her to discuss selling his first mortgage as a deed in lieu of foreclosure. After he accepted Lisa's offer, she negotiated with Wachovia to make Randy's payments on the first mortgage. When that happened, Randy moved out of the property, and Lisa owned it outright.

Another option would have been for Lisa to wait until the property went into foreclosure, in which case, she might have been able to buy it on the courthouse steps, maybe even for less money than she had paid to buy out the second and first mortgages, but then she would have had to evict Randy.

Lisa initially found this property through the company that held the second mortgage, which was trying to sell off its pool of second loans. The company ran an ad in a newspaper called *I Wanna* (www.iwanna.com) in North Carolina. Lisa met with them and selected Randy's mortgage from what they were offering to sell. The second mortgage was for $20,000, and Lisa bought it for $4,000. We've found that buying second mortgages is a great way to acquire investment properties. Lisa held this property for about two years and then sold it when real estate prices in the area started to rise. Moreover, Lisa financed the sale for the buyer, and she carried the payments at 12½ percent for five years, which was another great deal for her. When she bought the property, it was valued at $129,000 and had only $79,000 left on the mortgage, so her cost was even less. She sold it two years later for $260,000—more than three times the price she paid. In the current real estate market, these deals are common and their numbers are growing.

Buying Properties in Foreclosure

In 2008, the number of foreclosures in the United States skyrocketed. Foreclosures are properties that have been repossessed, usually because the owner is financially unable to make the mortgage payments, is several months in arrears, and is unable to negotiate new mortgage terms with the bank holding the mortgage. These homeowners then incur fees, in addition to what they already owe to their lenders, so they lose their property.

Locating a foreclosure in the current market is a lot easier than it ever has been because the number of foreclosures is on the rise. You can find foreclosed properties listed by city and state by checking out the Web sites of such government agencies as the Department of Housing and Urban Development (www.hud.gov) and the Department of Veterans Affairs (www.va.gov). You can also check the Web sites for Fannie Mae (www.fanniemae.com) and Freddie Mac (www.freddiemac.com). Or consider banks, credit unions, real estate agents, Internet subscription services, auction companies, and even craigslist (www.craigs list.org)—they all have listings of foreclosures.

Before you even start looking for specific properties in foreclosure, however, be aware that at the time of this writing certain states have passed laws, or are considering laws, on foreclosures. Check with the department of real estate in the state where you're interested in buying a foreclosure to make sure you're up to date with current legislation.

What to Look Out for When Buying Foreclosures

If a property has been foreclosed and the bank has already taken it back (in this case, the property is typically referred to as *real estate owned* or REO), you usually go through a real estate company that handles the negotiation on behalf of you, the purchaser. Before pursuing this type of investment, there are some issues you should be aware of.

REO properties are listed "as is" when they've been taken back by the bank, which means that after you close on the property, you have no recourse for any damages or defects on the home. To avoid any surprises, after you close your deal, have the property inspected by a professional home inspector. We can't emphasize that enough because we've seen foreclosed properties in terrible condition.

For instance, our accountant, Haimy, bought a property in foreclosure last year. Because she had no real estate investing experience and had no idea what she was looking at, we helped her through the process. She wanted to live in a specific area outside of San Francisco. She couldn't afford to buy in 2007 because the houses were selling in the mid-$400,000s. In 2008, a house that had been on the market in 2007 for $400,000 went into foreclosure and was priced to sell at $270,000. After the property was absolutely foreclosed on and the bank had had no bites from anybody, it went into REO status and was listed with a real estate agent who handled REO properties.

Haimy was able to buy that property at $242,000 in a bid process, and she bought it as is. After the property was hers, we went with her to look at it, and it was a disaster. It had holes in the floors and the walls. The wiring was pulled out of the walls. Most of the windows had been boarded up because the kids in the neighborhood threw rocks at the house and had broken all the windows. All the appliances were gone. The toilet was on the floor. The tiles from the bathroom were broken. Yet Haimy thought she was getting a good deal!

We advised her to have a home inspector come out to get an idea of what she was in for. Fortunately, the home inspector found nothing *structurally* wrong with the house, and he determined that the roof was new, the water heater wasn't in bad condition, and there was no evidence of mold or lead or any other environmental problems. However, the property needed an enormous amount of repair work. We estimated that her fix-up costs alone would be more than $50,000, and that's if she did it on the cheap!

But for Haimy, this was a good deal because she couldn't have afforded a $400,000 property in the neighborhood where she wanted to live. However, that property was a good deal only because Haimy's husband, Michael, can fix almost anything, and he's doing all the repairs and renovations himself. If they had to pay professionals to repair that property, it wouldn't have been cost effective. So that type of deal might be appealing to homeowners who are willing to live in a home while renovating it themselves, but from an investor's standpoint, buying properties that need a lot of work is a different story. Although a purchase price of $242,000 could be a good deal, you also need to calculate the repairs and the lack of cash flow while you're fixing up the property. If you have to do extensive repairs and renovations, obviously you won't be making any money on that investment until it's ready to rent out or sell.

With any real estate investment, you should evaluate the total cost associated with the property before you buy it—because "as is" means *as is*. Consider repairs, insurance, taxes, and the potential profit from a future sale, whenever that future sale may be. If you're looking at the long term, you've got to factor the long term. How much longer is it going to take you to realize a gain? And don't count on a quick flip.

Financing Foreclosures as Investments

Some lenders are willing to make loans to help people buy foreclosed properties, but others are not. Take the time and do the research necessary to find a lender willing to work with you specifically. Here are a few tips to help get financing for a foreclosure.

First, get prequalified, because walking into a deal with a loan preapproved is better than walking in with nothing. Foreclosures usually have several people bidding on a property, so being prequalified could make the difference and single you out as a desirable buyer. Keep in mind that 9 times out of 10, a lender is going to sell to an owner-occupant rather than to an investor, so the more attractive you as an investor can make yourself to the lender, the better your chances are of buying that property.

If you're interested in assuming the seller's loans, some loans allow you to do that, others do not. In this market, more banks are flexible. If you want to assume a loan, always try to negotiate with the seller's institution.

If you have equity in your current home, you can try to tap into that and take out a home equity loan to purchase a foreclosure as an investment, but we don't recommend that in the current market for two reasons. First, getting a home equity line of credit at the time of this writing is difficult. Second, we believe in being as debt free as possible or at least having a strong debt-to-equity balance. We feel that people should tap into the equity on their own property only for emergencies and not to buy investment property or any other investments.

Finally, consider working with a private lender as an investment partner. In the current market, investors have many opportunities to obtain a quality property at a discounted price. If you want to take advantage of these opportunities but are tight on cash, finding a private lender could be your ticket.

Doing Due Diligence on Foreclosures

After a foreclosure, the homeowners always have a redemption period during which they can pay back the total fees and payments and reclaim the property. Many investors aren't aware of this—they believe that they own the property free and clear after they have bought it on the courthouse steps.

In the current market, the chances of a homeowner reclaiming a property during the redemption period are very low. However, it is not unheard of, so take redemption periods into account.

When you're doing your due diligence in buying a foreclosure, check for any liens that are attached to the property. You would be amazed by what you find, and the IRS trumps everyone. If the IRS puts a lien against the property, that lien must be paid off before the property can be sold. You want to have clear title, so make sure that there are no mechanic's liens or construction liens or any other issues left over from the owner prior to the foreclosure.

Finally, when you're buying from distressed sellers, keep in mind that this is an emotional issue for them. Although on one hand, sellers are eager to sell the property to get out from under debt, they are typically not happy about the situation they're in. In many of the foreclosures currently on the market, people are literally giving up their properties and moving across the street and renting a property from somebody else. For the seller, this is usually an emotional process, so we recommend that you be careful and cautious when dealing with distressed sellers.

Buyer Beware: Lender Deficiency Judgments

If you're buying a short sale, a foreclosure, or a deed in lieu of foreclosure, be aware that the seller's lender can file a deficiency judgment against the seller for the difference between the amount the home sells for (to you, as the investor) at auction or short sale and what is owed, plus the lender's attorney's fees and court fees. This can happen in several states.

For example, New Jersey is a deficiency judgment state, which means that the lender can go after other assets that the seller has to make up the shortfall on the lender's investment to the seller. It's very important when you're buying a property in this situation that the seller is *completely absolved* of financial responsibility. Moreover, even if the lender agrees to forgive the debt and not file a deficiency judgment against the seller, the IRS might still want its cut because it views the forgiven debt as income.

Buying Judgments against Homeowners

Buying judgments is another way you can buy property, and it provides a regular cash flow. It might take you a long time to collect, but you can pick up judgments against other people's judgments for pennies on the dollar.

To find judgments, all you need to do is go to your local courthouse. When somebody files a judgment against a property, it becomes a matter of public record. So let your fingers do the walking in the registry of deeds office, the land recorder's office, or any public records office that your local courthouse directs you to. You can then read through the records to see who has a judgment. You can then send the person that is holding the judgment a letter saying something like, "I buy judgments for cash. You don't have to worry about ever getting paid out of a bankruptcy or any other type of small claims judgment. I'll be happy to buy that for cash."

If your offer is agreeable, that person benefits by getting a lump sum from you immediately for the total amount of the judgment (at a discount, of course, which is how you, the investor, make your money). The judgment holder doesn't have to wait 1 year, or 5 years, or 10 years to get paid under the terms of that case. And *you* benefit because you increase your cash flow. For instance, if you buy a judgment for 20 cents on the dollar, it's quite likely that with only one or two letters, you might get paid back 50 cents on the dollar.

In a way, you're becoming a collection agency, but you're also parlaying your money with the collection of real debt. Buying judgments is a big business. For example, we know of an investor named Jimmy who buys judgments in Chipley, a very rural area in northwestern Florida. Jimmy goes to the Chipley courthouse and researches who has judgments—against real estate or any other situation in which someone is owed money. Jimmy started buying judgments in the mid-1970s, and he paid 20 to 25 cents on the dollar for each judgment.

After he bought a judgment, Jimmy often sent a strong letter to the person who the judgment was filed against saying something like this: "Govern yourself accordingly that I do have the judgment. If you would like to negotiate to get this judgment off your books, we can discuss the possibility of my buying this judgment from you so that when you sell your house, you will have already satisfied your debt." The person could then decide whether to negotiate with Jimmy. The worst that could happen to Jimmy is that he would have to wait until the person eventually sold the house or business. Jimmy would have to be paid back at that time, because the property or business owner couldn't sell it if there was a lien against it.

One thing to keep in mind in the judgment business is that you must renew the lien periodically because, in general, liens last for only about five years. You can renew a lien with the local government agency where you have the judgment, which you can do by e-mail. You can't renew by phone because you have to sign a document. You can fax the document in, and the courthouse clerks can tell you exactly what they're looking for.

Generally, in today's market, you will be able to buy judgments and then negotiate with the person whom the judgment is against. This is especially true if that person is trying to sell real estate, because the seller must give clean title to whoever is trying to buy the property. In fact, collecting on judgments has become *easier* in this market, not more difficult. Again, the worst that can happen is that you might need to hold onto the judgment for a while until the person sells the property or business.

BUYING TAX LIENS

Another investment possibility is buying tax liens. Government agencies (generally the country or municipality where a property is located) can put liens against properties on which taxes are owed. Given the current state of the economy, more and more tax delinquencies are occurring. Typically, a county sells tax liens at auction to individual investors. The government agency sells the liens because it needs money to pay for the fire department, the police department, and other services that it provides to its residents. For example, Philadelphia was recently in the news because it had so many delinquent taxes that it had almost no revenue, so its mayor asked the federal government for a buyout.

Buying tax liens is also another way to acquire property because if the taxes are never reclaimed, fixed, or redeemed to pay off the investor, the investor is then able to buy that property at a discount.

Each state and municipality has its own way of handling tax liens. Some are bid based on a type of lottery system, whereby a numbered ball pops up and the bidder who has the matching number is given the option to buy that tax lien. Others are based on a bid-down system in which the bidding might start at 18 percent interest, but if many people bid on that lien, the interest rate continues to go down. The interest is what the county pays to the investor over a specified period of time while the investor is waiting to collect. In effect, what you're doing is paying off that property owner's delinquent tax to the county and, in return, you're paid an interest rate when that lien is satisfied.

Redemption periods on these liens can range anywhere from three to six months to three years. These are good investments if you have only a small amount of money to invest. They're also excellent investments via your IRA. The benefit of investing in liens is that you typically receive a much higher interest rate than you would by investing in bonds or even stocks. For example, Arizona offers a maximum rate of 16 percent, and both Florida and Wyoming offer a maximum of 18 percent. There's generally a minimum rate, usually in the neighborhood of 5 percent, which is currently higher than what you can get in a money market account, CD, or other type of savings account.

Tax liens are usually publicized as legal notices in the local newspaper, approximately six to eight weeks prior to the tax lien sale. That gives you the opportunity to look at the property and assess whether it is something that you would want to buy the lien on.

Be cautious, though: Stay away from anything with environmental issues, hazards, and if it looks like it's been condemned. In such situations, the chances are that the owners of that property are never going to see the day when their tax liens are satisfied, and then you'll be the proud owner of a property that could have many thousands of dollars' worth of problems. So, again, *be careful, do your due diligence, and check out the property before you invest.*

If you're buying tax liens in a state where you don't live, find someone in that state who can check out the property for you, even if you have to pay that person a fee. Find someone who knows the area and its different neighborhoods and can tell you more than you could possibly find out from afar.

Tax liens are a great way to invest with very few dollars. If property taxes in North Carolina are, for example, $1,000 a year, and a property owner has not paid the property taxes, the city or county is going to auction that lien. Lisa has bought tax liens in Wyoming for $300, and you could buy a tax lien for as low as $200, depending on what the lien is.

Natrona County, which is where Casper, Wyoming, is located, does a tax lien auction every year. About six weeks before the auction, the county advertises in the local paper all the properties that have delinquent taxes. When Lisa wanted to make this type of investment, she paid a real estate agent she knew who lived there to try to get inside the properties to be auctioned. She asked him to get as much information about the properties and the area as possible. The real estate agent sent Lisa quite a bit of information. Lisa found a property that she was interested in, so she drove up there and looked at it. She wanted to know before she invested in it whether it was in an area that she wanted to own the tax lien. If she had to later sue and got the tax deed as a result, she would be able to buy that property, so she wanted to be sure that it was something she would be interested in owning.

Lisa has bought a few tax liens in Natrona County, each costing between $200 and $800. All of them are secured by single-family houses that have tax delinquencies against them. In some cases, these single-family houses have been free and clear with no mortgage, but the owners didn't pay their taxes. Two of these cases were estate situations in which the owners had passed away and the heirs had not thought about the taxes on the property. Lisa sent the estate a letter offering to pay off the taxes on the property. Because the new owners hadn't realized that there were taxes owed on the property, Lisa's letter obviously got their attention quickly. The new owners went to the county office and paid off their tax liens, and Lisa got paid off at 18 percent. So she made $200 plus 18 percent. That might not seem like a lot of money, but if you're buying multiple tax liens, or if you don't have a lot of cash and these are properties located in your backyard, they are great little investments to make. In addition, you can make them through your IRA.

Lisa started buying tax liens when she was looking to buy some real estate in Wyoming. At that time, she lived in Colorado, about 45 minutes from the Wyoming border. She thought Wyoming was a great investing opportunity because real estate was reasonably priced, it was a great retirement area, there was no state income tax, and property taxes were very low—all of which made it a great area to rent property to people who were retiring there. She decided it would be a good market, with not a lot of competition.

One downside was that not a lot of people were living there, so Lisa realized she should investigate what would be the best way to acquire real estate. She met a few investors in Cheyenne who had been actively purchasing tax liens. She found out about the Cheyenne group from a real estate investor group that she belonged to. Networking is the way we do almost everything. Through her connections, she learned how to buy liens at auctions.

Every state handles its tax liens differently, and we've been to only a few auctions. To make this type of investment, investigate how liens are handled where you are interested in investing. For example, in Mariposa County, Arizona, you can now bid online, but in Wyoming, you have to be there in person, you need identification, and you must have certified funds on deposit.

The first lottery she attended in Natrona County was held in the courthouse in a conference room that was part of the treasurer's office. To enter the lottery room, Lisa had to first register with the treasurer's office, and they verified that Lisa had certified funds (for that particular lottery, she had $10,000). She went with people with whom she had connected with in Cheyenne to help walk her through the process because it was her first lottery.

About 60 people were there. The person in charge of the lottery called out the address of a property and rolled the lottery ball (just as you see on TV). If the ball was Lisa's number, she could choose to buy that tax lien. At the end of the auction, you go back to the treasurer's office, which processes your sale and gives you a certificate.

About 150 properties were auctioned, and the lottery lasted the entire afternoon. Lisa stayed until the end because she didn't want to miss anything. She wanted to see exactly how the process worked, and she wanted to ask questions of the people she had gone with—for example, she wanted to know why particular liens didn't sell. In many cases, liens didn't sell because of environmental issues or legal complications. For example, Wyoming has a lot of oil and mineral deposits, and some of the properties being auctioned were near a mineral field. Other properties had water rights issues that investors didn't want to deal with. The next day,

Lisa drove around with the list of properties that had been offered and sold so she could see them for herself. That way she would know the next time how to save time and effort when considering this type of alternative investment.

If the logistics involved in checking out this type of investment are difficult for you, you might be able to get help with it. The best thing you can do is to find somebody who lives or works in the area. You pay that person for assistance in doing your due diligence. Or you could go with that person to learn the ropes so that both of you learn how to make this type of deal and develop an alliance to work on them together.

Wyoming uses a combined lottery and auction system, but many states use auctions without lotteries. For example, Florida holds auctions, where the officials start at a certain price, and investors can bid on the same property. Some states, such as Texas, don't make liens; instead, they sell tax deeds. If you buy the tax deed, you can redeem it in exchange for the property itself. Check out the laws in the state you're interested in, which you can do through that state's department of real estate.

Although you can acquire a property by first buying the tax lien against it, Lisa hasn't done that. Instead, she has always been paid off 100 percent. However, with the recent downturn in the real estate market, it will be interesting to see if people are getting paid off on the liens. Liens are typically for such small amounts of money that the investors probably are getting paid off. Moreover, if property owners are in situations in which their mortgage companies or lenders are responsible for keeping the taxes and insurance in escrow, those property owners will definitely pay off the tax liens because they want to protect their equity. A tax lien is in a senior position to a lender. In other words, the property owner must pay off a tax lien before selling the property. That's why tax liens are so valuable and why you get paid off 9 times out of 10. They're very good debt instruments.

Areas like Arizona and Florida have higher-priced liens because the real estate taxes are higher. Therefore, buying tax liens in Wyoming, where the real estate taxes are less than $1,000 a year on average, will be slightly different from buying tax liens in California, where the real estate taxes on average are $4,000 to $5,000, or in Florida, where it's common to see $3,000 in taxes on a $150,000 property.

We like investing in tax liens and tax deeds because they're simple and there's not as much competition as there is with other real estate investments. Lisa was making this type of investment from 1995 until 2003. The only reason she stopped was that she got busy with other investments. But if we had the time and if the properties were in an area we knew well, we would still be making them. Before you make this type of investment, find out the interest rate that the government will pay. In nearly all cases, it will be much higher than what you could make in any other type of investment that requires such a small amount of money. They're also a great way to acquire a property that you want to own for a very reasonable price. This type of investment is a great way to make a good return on your investment, and it's a relatively safe investment, even in today's economy.

BUYING TAX DEEDS

Another type of alternative investment is to buy the deed and own the real estate. The process for buying a tax deed is different from buying a tax lien in that when you buy a tax deed, you get the actual deed. A government agency sells a tax deed when it forces the sale of a property for nonpayment of taxes. It is one of two methods government agencies use to collect delinquent taxes owned on real estate (the other is a tax lien sale). County, municipal, and state governments differ on how they handle properties on which taxes are owed. For example, Florida sells tax liens on such properties, whereas Texas sells tax deeds.

Generally, the redemption period for a tax deed is shorter than for a tax lien. For instance, in Texas, a property owner has six months to pay back the delinquent taxes. If the property owner hasn't paid the taxes within that time, the investor who bought the tax deed can sue to acquire the property. To get information on tax deed sales in your area, contact your state treasurer's office or department of real estate.

Acquiring tax deeds are buyer-beware sales because the properties are sold as is. So, again, it's vitally important that you know what you're buying before you buy it. Personally, we have never invested in tax deeds primarily because the states that we've always invested in aren't tax deed states; they are tax lien states. Our personal strategy is to invest only in states we know well, which is where we've lived. If you are interested in tax deed investments, check out the local real estate investors associations. In states like Texas and Georgia, these investor groups have experienced tax deed investors among their members.

Buying Properties on a Lease Option Basis

As this book was being written, there were changes in real estate laws and regulations being proposed or enacted in almost every state, county, and municipality. It has been amazing to see the lengths to which some state and local government agencies have gone to try to collect revenues. For example, some cities are now charging fees to be a landlord—a landlord license! These fees are like business license fees per investment property. Milwaukee does this already, and Cincinnati is considering this practice. You must consider pending law and regulation changes in your investment philosophy as well as your cash flow. The best place to find out what is happening in your state is to visit the secretary of state's office where you are trying to acquire property. There or through the state's department of real estate, you can learn if lease options are legal and which fees are associated with owning investment property.

A lease option is a popular technique to help investors tie up real estate for a period of time without putting a lot of money into the deal. A lease option is a relatively simple contract that is appended to a lease. It states that the property owner agrees to sell the property in the specified circumstances to the person renting the property—that is, the person signing the lease. The option is the contract that fixes the price of the property for a certain period of time, which the person buying the property can capitalize on.

If you're the *buyer*, you want the time frame of that option agreement to be as long as possible, especially in this market. If the value of that property has gone down recently, and if you can get an option contract for 10 years at today's price, chances are that 10 years from now the property will be worth a whole lot more money. Obviously, for the same reason, if you're the *seller*, you want the time frame of that option agreement to be as short as possible.

In the current real estate market, an unusually high number of sellers are willing to option their properties. Most of these sellers are primarily interested in covering their mortgage payments. If that is the case for the seller you are working with, you can probably negotiate any term you want.

For example, right now, Lisa is negotiating a 10-year option agreement with a seller for a property that she is willing to buy eventually. If that seller accepts Lisa's option agreement, she will sublease the property. She already has a tenant who is interested. Lisa will lease the property on a yearly basis because she believes that the inventory of rental properties in this market will eventually decrease. She has made this prediction based on the high number of properties that are already in foreclosure to which even more foreclosures will be added in the near future, despite what the government does to try to slow the rate of foreclosures. People who have lost their homes still need a place to live, so they will become renters, which will reduce the available inventory of rentals in good neighborhoods. Moreover, if inflation continues to increase (which economists say it will), rents will increase as well.

Another example of a lease option property that we know about is a single-family house in an over-55 community. Lisa knows an investor—let's call him Joe—from California who bought a property in Ocala, Florida, two years ago for $235,000. Joe has tried to sell it for the last nine months, but he has not gotten one bite—not even at $175,000. Of course, if Joe sold it for only $175,000, he would take a severe loss, and he would have to bring cash to the table just to pay off his mortgage. Joe has tried everything to sell it. He listed it with a real estate agent for three months, and then he put it on the Internet and tried to sell it himself. He even went to Florida to attend a meeting of a local real estate investors association to talk to people there in hopes of finding somebody to take it off his hands.

But Joe couldn't find anybody who was interested for two reasons. First, the market has gone down significantly in that area; and second, his property is in an over-55-year-old community, which reduces the market of potential buyers. Moreover, many people who are moving to Florida prefer to lease for a while to make sure that they really want to live there. Because of the hurricanes, sink holes, and other environmental factors in Florida, everybody's a little bit more cautious about buying. Florida is one of the top states that has taken a beating in the real estate market. But poor Joe really needs to get rid of this property, and he can't.

Lisa offered to lease his property with an option at $175,000 for 10 years. She also offered to give him a fee, called an *option consideration*, which in this case was $1,000. If he agreed to the deal, Lisa would have 10 years to buy this property for $175,000, and her rent payment to Joe will be exactly the same price as his mortgage payment, which is $1,200 per month. This arrangement works for Lisa because she knows someone from Michigan who wants to live in Ocala from January to May, because Ocala is the capital of horse country in Florida. Horse people celebrate the Horse Shows in the Sun (HITS) season during that time. Lisa's Michigan tenant is willing to pay her $1,450 in rent per month (so Lisa will make a small profit in the rental income each month), and the tenant is willing to pay for the entire year, even though she's only going to be living in the property for about 5½ months. She's wealthy, but she doesn't want to buy property nor does she want to live in a hotel from January until the end of May. On top of that, keep in mind that if there are any maintenance problems or any other problems with the property, those are Joe's responsibility because he's still the legal owner.

As of this writing, Joe is still considering Lisa's offer, and he may come back and ask for more time on the option consideration or for more money. But Lisa is not willing to option the property for more than $175,000 because Joe can't even sell it for $175,000. If he agrees to the lease option, Lisa will hold the option to buy for 10 years. If, during that period of time, the property increases in value, or if Lisa finds a buyer who is willing to pay her more than $175,000, Lisa can buy the property from Joe for $175,000. What makes this a terrific investment is that Lisa can buy into this property for only $1,000. She can also assign that contract to somebody else and make money. For example, suppose two years from now, Lisa finds buyers and the property is now worth $190,000. She could sell them her contract for $10,000, and those buyers could then buy the property for $175,000. The new buyer would get a $5,000 discount on the property's market value, and Lisa would make $10,000 on her original $1,000 investment.

That's why we see lease options as a great alternative investment right now. The worst that can happen is that your tenant falls through and you need to find another tenant. If that happened to Lisa, she would have to pay $1,200 a month to Joe until she found another tenant. However, she's not worried about that because she knows she could market the property in this particular neighborhood successfully because of the number of people who own thoroughbred horses and want to be in Ocala for five months a year to show their horses.

How to Find Lease Option Opportunities

Lisa found Joe, the owner of the Ocala property, where we live in California among our network of investors. One of our friends said she had a friend in serious financial trouble, and she asked Lisa if we could help. Lisa was willing to help, but it had to be a win-win situation for both Lisa and Joe.

The lease option is a win for Joe because Lisa is paying his mortgage, so he doesn't have that weight around his neck every month. It is a win for Lisa because she has an option to buy the property from Joe for 10 years for only $175,000, even if the property increases in value. Joe can't sell the property without Lisa's permission and her negating her contract. Joe is guaranteed to receive $175,000, even if the property's value continues to decrease. Of course, the opposite might also happen. If the property *increases* in value, and if somebody offers him, say, $250,000 for the house, Joe could try to get Lisa to assign her contract back to him. If she agrees, Joe pays Lisa a fee for doing that—for example, he might offer her $10,000. In that case, Lisa still makes $10,000 on her original investment of $1,000. And if Lisa's subtenant pays her $1,450 per month, she'll make $250 each month on the rental.

That's why we like lease options. If you're in a down market, lease options are great alternative investments for you, and they are also beneficial for the person you're buying from, as long as you can make the deal a win.

One cautionary note: If the seller has to pay any monthly fees to make the deal good, we caution you *against* agreeing to that lease option. For example, you need to make sure that the seller's mortgage is really being paid because if it isn't and the seller goes into foreclosure, you can lose your option to buy. To protect yourself, you must have an option agreement *in writing*, and it needs to be fair to both parties. You might want to consult with an attorney or have your attorney draw up the legal documents specifically for your situation (and in this market, we recommend that). A property is a significant asset, and legal representation is not very expensive in comparison—maybe only a few hundred dollars. That is money well spent, especially if you are interested in buying more lease options in the future. Also, make sure the option and lease are separate agreements with the seller and that your lease with your subtenant is another separate agreement.

Lisa has entered into lease options as both a buyer and a seller. She has entered into many lease options through corporations and relocation companies, especially when the relocation company needs to relocate somebody in a down real estate market. In those situations, the relocation company can't get much money for the property. Selling the property on a lease option basis allows the company to move the person without waiting for the real estate market to improve. In a down market, lease options are a good way to go.

How to Find Subtenants for Single-Family Homes

You don't have to find a community like Ocala, Florida, to be able to rent out a house. There's a market of people who want to rent houses in almost every area of the country. Many people think of rentals as part of an apartment complex. Yet there are many reasons why people want to rent a single-family house. Some people can't afford to buy, or their credit isn't perfect, or they don't meet the debt-to-income ratios that lenders require, or they can't get conventional financing. These people still want to live in a single-family house in a nice neighborhood. Some people believe that the real estate market is going to continue to go down, so they don't want to buy *yet* because they're concerned that they'll lose money on their investment. And then some people may have already been foreclosed on, and they need to rent because they are unable to buy another property.

As a real estate investor, you also need to keep in mind that some people who rent are not too concerned about the condition of the property they're renting. The downside of this type of real estate investment is that some renters have turned really nice properties into problem properties that need work. In these cases, the property values have actually decreased because of the number of distressed rentals in those areas. But that doesn't mean you shouldn't invest in real estate as rental property. Rather, it means that you need to be very careful about whom you're renting to.

If you're buying a property on a lease option basis and renting it out during the term of the lease option with the ultimate goal being that you want to live in that property yourself, you should take the long view. In our case, if we loved the area in which a property was located, and if we knew the area well and what the property was worth, we would buy it because the price wouldn't really matter 5 or 10 years from now if that was a place we wanted to live in. A lease option is a great way to invest in property like that.

In 1990, Lisa bought a home in Fort Collins, Colorado, on a one-year lease option basis. The seller was a pilot for USAir. He needed to move to Pittsburgh for his job. He couldn't sell his property because the market in Fort Collins at that time was very weak. Lisa was moving from North Carolina to Fort Collins. Because that move would be a really big change, she wanted to see if she liked Fort Collins before settling there permanently. The neighborhood that she was interested in had no rentals. This was a community of homeowners, not renters. She offered to buy the pilot's home, with a $5,000 option consideration, for $105,000. After a year, Lisa had an option to buy the property. If she didn't buy it, the pilot would keep her $5,000. He received monthly rent payments from Lisa. This deal had no rent credits, which is a portion of the rent money that each month is put toward a down payment on the house.

During the course of that year, the pilot wrote to Lisa, asking to buy her out of her lease option agreement. The first time he asked, he had a buyer who was willing to buy the property outright from him, but Lisa turned down his offer. The seller couldn't force her to cancel the agreement because she had worked with an attorney to make sure that she had legal documentation from the state of Colorado that was binding. The seller had no choice but to try to buy her out on the agreed-upon terms. He offered Lisa $5,000 if she would agree to nullify the agreement. If she had entered this lease option as an investor and not as an owner-occupant, she would have considered his offer, but because she had moved her family there and she needed a place to live, she said she couldn't do that. The seller asked Lisa two more times if she would consider selling the property because, within the year, it had become more marketable. But Lisa refused, and she exercised her option to buy the property for $105,000 under the terms of the original lease option. She sold it six years later for close to double the amount she had originally paid for it.

However, you don't have to *live* in the property you buy on a lease option basis. We've bought many properties as investors and then rented them out, but we're careful to whom we rent. For example, in Lisa's case, if Lisa hadn't wanted to live in the Fort Collins house, it would not have been a problem for her to find a great tenant in that community because it is a desirable residential area. She could have simply contacted Hewlett-Packard, which is just one of the companies located there, and asked if she could put up a flyer on their bulletin board or run an ad in the company newsletter saying, "We have a property for rent in a beautiful area in an exclusive neighborhood. The house has three bedrooms, three baths, and a fenced-in yard, and it is within walking distance to an elementary school on private bicycle walks. Discount rent. Call this number." That's exactly how we would advertise a property for rent.

The difficulty of renting out property lies in the due diligence of finding suitable tenants. We screen prospective tenants very thoroughly before we rent a property to them. In fact, we look for tenants who are not people renting a starter home. Also, the first thing we do in any type of rental situation—whether it's a lease option on a property we might live in someday or it's a property strictly for rental purposes—is to meet all the neighbors around the property. We give them our telephone number and say, "If you have any problems whatsoever with this tenant, please call us." And we've never, ever had a problem with neighbors. In fact, they appreciate knowing who the landlord is. We've never received a letter from a homeowners association saying that the yard is not being taken care of or any other problems.

If you are interested in buying property on a lease option basis, try to negotiate the term of the option to be as long as possible. And conversely, if you're selling a property to a buyer on a lease option basis, try to keep the term as short as you can. If you're the seller, try to get as much money down as you possibly can from the buyer and also take a security deposit toward the rent. In other words, have a separate accounting that goes with the lease.

Buying Properties out of Bankruptcy

The first thing you need to know about buying property out of bankruptcy is that a large percentage of people or business owners in foreclosure also file bankruptcy to stop the foreclosure. They file for bankruptcy in federal court, which stops any state court foreclosure, thus giving the homeowner or business owner some breathing room and a chance to reorganize his financial assets. The bank that holds the mortgage cannot continue with the foreclosure while the bankruptcy is active. But what ends up happening is that the bankruptcy court has a problem with the case and it consequently negates the bankruptcy. Then the homeowner or business owner gets foreclosed on anyway, so filing for bankruptcy really just delays the inevitable.

There's a small, quiet world of real estate investing in bankruptcies that doesn't capture the attention of the average investor, which is why bankruptcy can be an interesting way to buy property. Investing in bankruptcies is usually for the long term because flipping the property won't really be feasible. After all, if the original owner couldn't sell the property in the first place and is using bankruptcy only to stall foreclosure, you're not likely to be able to sell that property in the near term either. But you can still get a great deal. However, it can be difficult to discover the price because the seller is in bankruptcy, which is a court process. At the time of this writing, federal legislation is pending whereby bankruptcy judges can modify the local interest rate to make it more affordable for the borrower who has opted to file bankruptcy to keep the home.

BUYING PROPERTIES AT AUCTION

Recently, auctions have become a popular way to buy property. Auction companies receive a fee for helping the property owner sell the property (just as they do for auctioning any other type of property). Many properties sold at auction are in foreclosure or bankruptcy. Some owners post their property with online auctions, and you can bid on the property online. At live auctions, you can go and see the property and then submit a sealed bid.

A common assumption is that auctions are a good place to buy, but that is not always true. We've noticed that people who buy properties cheaply have a harder time when they try to sell those properties. Typically, the properties stay on the market longer than properties that were bought at fair market prices and are then sold at fair market prices.

As with any auction, be careful to not bid too much: Don't overpay for a property. Always remember that your profits are made *when you buy*. Keep that in the back of your mind at all times, in all situations. Auctions sound like a great way to get a good deal, but they might not necessarily be. For example, suppose you're interested in a property at an auction that has a starting price of $200,000. The same exact house down the street is for sale for $225,000. The auctioned property has a lot more activity in terms of prospective buyers because it's $25,000 cheaper than the property that's for sale for $225,000. But in the end, you might get a better deal from the owner selling the house than you would get at the auction because the hubbub over the lower price might actually cause the price to go up. The $200,000 house might end up costing $250,000 or even $300,000, while the same house down the street can be bought directly from the owner with time to thoroughly inspect what is being offered.

Buying Properties out of Probate

Probate is the process of gathering the assets held in the name of a deceased person, paying the person's debts, and distributing the assets that remain in accordance with the person's will (or, if the deceased didn't leave a valid will, in accordance with the laws of the intestate succession). Probate property sales have been around for a long time.

We have bought notes secured by real estate through probate, and the usual way we found those was through estate attorneys who were handling the probate process and representing the estate. In addition to finding these opportunities through estate lawyers, you can also find probate property through the Multiple Listing Service (MLS, www. mls.com). The property isn't listed as probate property, but you can use the MLS to first find available property in the area in which you're interested in buying and then working through your local courthouse to determine which of those MLS-listed properties are currently in probate. This information is all a matter of public record.

Why are probate sales a good way to go? Because, generally speaking, when someone dies and leaves an estate to multiple heirs, they're not all going to agree on what to do with the property. Some may want to hold onto it, but usually there's at least one heir who wants cash, which means that the property needs to be sold.

Is a probate property a bargain? Not necessarily, although they do typically sell at a discount. Typically, the minimum offered is 90 percent of the appraised value of the property. In today's market, 90 percent might be too high, so you need to assess whether it's a good bargain. Personally, we like probate sales since (just as in buying properties out of bankruptcy) there isn't as much competition to find deals because most people don't know how to buy property out of probate. Most people assume that they can simply look in the local newspaper obituary section and then call the estate directly, but that's not how it works. Probate properties are usually sold and marketed through real estate agents that represent the seller—who, in the case of a probate sale, is the estate. The real estate agent probably was referred to sell the property by the estate attorney, which means that estate attorneys are great sources for finding probate properties. If you can find a probate property directly through an attorney, you might not have to pay a real estate agent's commission. That could be a great deal, and you might get the property below the 90 percent price.

You can also ask real estate agents if they know any agents who handle only probate properties. Then let these agents know that you're looking for these situations, and they'll come to you to see if you want to buy before they ask anybody else. You can also search public records.

It's very important that you know what you're getting yourself into with a probate property. As for other alternative real estate investment opportunities we've described, when you buy out of probate, you're buying the property as is. So get a contractor to make a home inspection and do as much due diligence as you can before you make an offer. You don't want to buy a property that was owned by somebody who had lived there for 50 years but had never done any work on the property.

After your offer is accepted, a court date is set and published, and you go to court to buy the property. The court always makes the sale public in case somebody wants to offer more. The key to buying out of probate is to avoid probate court by negotiating a deal before it gets to that stage. In our opinion, estate attorneys are willing to negotiate and want quick closings so that they can get paid. The main reason to consider probate properties is that you can acquire property at prices below market value, with little or no competition.

Buying Mobile Homes

Even more so than buying property out of probate, mobile homes (or manufactured homes) might be the best-kept investment secret in real estate. While many investors struggle to raise money to pay taxes on a single high-end regular piece of real estate, mobile homes are much easier to make money on because they're cheaper to buy. If they're not on the land, they're treated as *personal* real estate, not as *real* real estate. In other words, you pay taxes on that type of mobile home the same way you pay taxes on a car loan. But if you take the wheels off and permanently affix your mobile home to the land, it becomes real estate. Buying a mobile home is an easy investment requiring less money than other types of real estate, especially if you're in an area of the country where mobile homes are popular.

Many people assume that they'll find mobile homes only in the sunbelt states, such as Florida, Arizona, or California, but that's definitely not the case. Mobile home communities are all over the country. For example, Lisa's son Bill has bought mobile homes in a park in Mankato, Minnesota, which is freezing in the wintertime and often 40 degrees below zero. Of course, mobile homes in these climates are built a bit differently. They have better insulation for one thing.

Bill bought his first mobile home while he was still in college. The cost was only $7,000, and the home was part of an estate. A friend's grandfather had died, and the friend told Bill that the family had to decide what to do with all his grandfather's possessions, which included a mobile home. Bill was intrigued. He had not done any investing on his own yet, and he thought this was a manageable, low-cost first investment. The mobile home was located in a mobile home park. Bill negotiated with the park manager that, if the tenant in Bill's mobile home didn't make his monthly payments, Bill would guarantee payment for the lot.

In addition to his initial $7,000 purchase price, Bill invested another $2,500 into the home. He put in a new floor and brand-new appliances, and he spiffed up the place. He currently gets $550 a month for the mobile home, which includes the lot rent, and he then allocates the $150 lot rent to the mobile home park manager. So he's making $400 a month from this mobile home that he spent $9,500 on for as long as he wants to keep it. That's $4,800 a year. He broke even within the first two years He bought the home six years ago, so he has been earning $400 a month for the past four years, with few if any expenses. That's a *phenomenal* investment for someone who doesn't have a lot of money but who wants to continually get cash flow with a check every month.

Many people assume that mobile homes decrease in value over time. Although that's true to some extent, with the economy what it is right now, they are not decreasing as much in value. The key to buying a decent mobile home is to buy one that's less than 10 years old because the older the mobile home, the more electrical and other types of expenses you might have. If you are renting the lot for the home, some mobile park owners do not allow a mobile home that's more than 10 years old.

Some mobile home parks (for example, where Bill's mobile home is located) are small parks that limit the number of rentals. Most of the people who live in the park own their mobile homes, which is a comfortable situation for Bill. Because the mobile home park is located only two miles from Bill's own home, it's easy for him to manage with little upkeep required.

Of course, the most important factor if you're considering investing in mobile homes is to realize that this is an affordable housing option for many people who cannot afford
a house. If the tenant doesn't pay, it's pretty simple to evict
that person and find a new tenant. As the economy worsens,
more and more people around the country will be looking
at mobile homes as a workable option that's much more
affordable than conventional housing. After all, where else
can you pay $550 a month, total, for the cost of renting a
home and the lot it sits on? It's very hard for a tenant to find
a better deal than that.

Mobile homes also make a good investment for people
who want to use their IRA funds to invest in personal property,
not "real" real estate. Because they're low-priced investments,
you can continue to buy new ones to build wealth. For example, Bill now owns a few mobile homes, free and clear, all in
Minnesota. He found the others by contacting the park managers directly, asking if he can talk to any mobile home owners
who are trying to sell their mobile homes and can't. That offer
is beneficial to the mobile home park managers because they
continue to get lot rent if Bill buys the mobile homes.

As mentioned, Bill found this alternative investing opportunity by chance, but you don't need to wait for opportunities to just fall in your lap. There are a lot of places to buy
mobile homes, especially used ones. For example, you can
buy from an estate sale, as Bill did. You can contact mobile
home dealers and ask if they know people who are trading
in mobile homes for new ones. In most cases, those owners are happy to get rid of their old mobile homes and will
sell at a deep discount. You can also go online to the State
Mobile Home Manufacturing Housing Association, which
lists all the dealers in the state in which you're interested.
That Web site also lists associations in your state of active

mobile home investors, and you can join these associations and start networking.

The mobile home business will continue to grow. According to the 2000 census, almost 9 million mobile homes are in the United States—there were only 800,000 back in 1950. This is an excellent option if you are in an area of the country where mobile homes are acceptable. If you're interested in learning more, check out the wonderful book *Deals on Wheels* by Lonnie Scruggs. It has an enormous amount of information for investors who want to buy mobile homes or mobile home paper.

INVESTING IN MOBILE HOME PARKS

In addition to buying one or more mobile homes and renting them out, you might also consider investing in a mobile home park, which is the land and the homes that sit on the land. Lisa did this back in the late 1990s. She owned a very small park outside of Asheville, North Carolina. Lisa later sold the park when she moved to Colorado because it would have been too difficult to oversee that investment from so far away.

There are also investors who use a rent-to-own strategy, which is another way of buying mobile homes. For example, Lisa bought a mobile home for $2,000 and refurbished it for $500. She then sold it on a rent-to-own basis, whereby the tenant paid $450 a month for a five-year period, at the end of which the tenant owned the home outright.

The people who typically buy mobile homes on a rent-to-own basis are on fixed incomes, and they prefer to own their home instead of renting it. Mobile homes provide housing for many people who have low incomes or government-subsidized incomes. They want to live in a mobile home because there's little maintenance required. In Lisa's case, in the late 1990s, not one of her tenants would have been able to qualify for a regular loan. In terms of the quality of those tenants, some were good and rented for 10 years, and some were so bad that she paid them to move out. In the rental business, whether it is real estate, mobile homes, or horse trailers, you are not always guaranteed the best tenants, even if you do verify their applications. But then again, you're not always making a return in the stock market either.

Working with existing mobile home park managers is a great strategy if you are looking to buy just the home, not the land. You can easily identify the parks in which you would like to own homes and work out a deal with the park managers who end up watching your tenants for you. Believe us when we say that they will call you if your tenant is trouble. Mobile homes are one of the few investments available that provide positive cash flow. If you don't have a lot of money, or you don't have a lot of time, and you want a very easy investment, this is it.

There are a few things you need to watch out for when investing in mobile homes. First, you might need a license. You can call your city, state, or county licensing department to find out the licensing requirements—such as a dealer's license—if you buy more than one mobile home. Second, you want to find out whether there are any local zoning requirements that would prohibit you from buying a park and putting mobile homes on it. Check also whether there are any environmental issues that you might want to consider. For the most part, mobile homes are a good investment in many great areas of the country, in spite of tornadoes, hurricanes, and other natural disasters.

Another important due diligence factor in owning a mobile home park is to make sure that it has water and that the sources and lines are in good repair. You also need water meters. Make sure there are well-functioning wastewater disposal systems on the land itself if the park is not connected to a municipal sewage disposal system. Check out the gas lines and connections as well as all the roads inside the park. If you're buying an existing park, you need to get an inspection of all those utilities. Be sure to look at the floor plans too.

When you are researching the zoning laws, beyond existing regulations, look into what is happening in your particular area as far as zoning is concerned. Affordable housing is an increasingly important issue. If the economy continues to worsen, we're going to see the need for more and more affordable housing situations, just as we saw in the aftermath of Hurricane Katrina in New Orleans. In that case, the Federal Emergency Management Agency (FEMA) had to find or develop affordable housing, which it did, some of it as far away as Florida. To do so, FEMA allowed areas that might not previously have been zoned for mobile home park use to be rezoned so that mobile home parks could be developed for people who needed a place to live. In fact, the government even subsidized those parks.

If you're interested in buying a mobile home park, go to a local real estate investors association and network among the members. Find out if anyone is trying to buy a new park and is looking for money. That would be another great investment, with little work required on your part. Lisa bought the park she owned through a seller-financed note. She bought a second mortgage that was secured by the park. Then the people who were making the payments defaulted on their first mortgage, and she was able to assume the first mortgage and take over the park.

Obviously, buying a park is more complicated than simply buying a mobile home, which is why many people who have only a little bit of money to invest simply invest in the mobile homes themselves. If you buy only a mobile home, you don't need to worry about water rights, gas, roads, sewage, and so on because that has all been established and taken care of by the park owners, and any problems in those areas are the responsibility of the mobile home park owners.

Investing in Storage Unit Rentals

Another type of real estate you might want to consider investing in is storage units. These have excellent investment potential, whether investing by yourself or with a partner, and they are another relatively simple investment to pursue. Storage units are facilities where people store their things. For people who are moving to a smaller house or apartment, have a second home in a ski area or on the water, or just need extra space to keep the possessions they aren't using every day, storage units are a dream come true. Customers pay a rental price per month, depending on the size of the storage unit. Customers who don't pay are generally denied access to their storage units. Many storage facilities have gotten so sophisticated that they have computers that lock out nonpaying renters. The renters in these situations can't get past the chain fence or wire mesh that secures the building, or they can't get into their storage unit until they've paid the bill.

Unlike having "tenants and toilets" (which is a common expression among real estate investors who rent out houses, condos, townhomes, or apartments), storage units are a very straightforward and manageable investment. Nothing in the facility itself can get damaged and, in most cases, the facilities are made of concrete. However, some storage facilities in humid climates are temperature controlled or for people who need climate-controlled storage space.

With locations in every corner of the United States, you would think there is a lot of competition and market saturation, but you would be amazed at the number of storage units that are still being built. The market for self-storage unit rentals is still growing, especially in places like Florida, Arizona, and Nevada. For example, despite Florida's general economic downturn, people are still moving there because, among its other advantages, it has no state income tax and the cost of living is low. Many people are moving from bigger houses, and they may start out by renting until they get to know the various neighborhoods. While they are renting, they need a space to store their things until they decide where they're going to settle permanently.

Investors tend to start out by buying older, relatively small facilities that need a little bit of upkeep and repair. These properties are generally not on the radar screen, and the big companies that own storage facilities (such as Extra Space Storage) aren't typically interested in them. So if you're looking to buy a business, you might consider investing in storage facilities, because they provide great positive cash flow, as well as *much less maintenance* than anything else you can buy. It really doesn't get any better than investing in this type of real estate.

Other low-maintenance opportunities are mailbox rental facilities, RV and boat parking spaces, and other areas where people are renting space that's not necessarily real estate. In that sense, these investment options are like buying mobile homes in that there's very little damage someone can do to the parking lot where the mobile home is located; similarly, there's very little damage a renter can do to a storage facility. For investors who don't want to be landlords per se but want to make a higher return on their money than other investments might offer, these facilities are an alternative.

Lisa's friend Nancy invested with five other private investors and bought a small mom-and-pop storage facility just outside of Memphis, Tennessee. The purchase price of the entire facility was just under $300,000. Nancy's investment was $50,000. This facility consisted of 48 storage units of different sizes, with rents ranging from $39.95 a month to $100 a month. It had a good enough cash flow for the group to pay a property manager to manage the facility for them. This passive investment is still in Nancy's portfolio.

The self-storage industry is one of the fastest-growing sectors in the United States. In recent years, the gross annual revenues have been around $22 billion. About 28,850 small business entrepreneurs own and operate just a single storage facility—and those small business people make up 90 percent of all self-storage facilities in the United States. You don't have to be part of a huge national company; instead, you can buy or build just one at a time. No matter where you are in the United States, storage facilities are in demand. So do your research: drive around, look in the Yellow Pages, or go online to see how many storage facilities are in your neighborhood. There may be an opportunity to invest in a self-storage facility that is a no-brainer, requires no upkeep, and can be a great cash cow.

As an investment, you might decide to build one or simply buy one from someone else. If you are considering buying one already built, negotiate your price; you can even ask for seller financing. You can find these opportunities by working with a business broker or contacting your local chapter of the Self-Storage Association (SSA). These groups have little communities, and you can usually find what's for sale through their publications.

CHAPTER

8

INVESTING IN BUSINESS-TO-BUSINESS CASH FLOWS

Investing in business-to-business cash flows makes sense for investors who are interested in acquiring investments outside of real estate and want to make investments they know, understand, can monitor, and can have some control over. The investments may or may not require active management. These investments are generally in the form of private loans or purchases of seller-financed business notes, secured by inventory or the business itself.

INVESTING IN CAR PAPER

One way to invest in a business-to-business cash flow is to buy what's called *car paper*. Back in the mid-1990s, Lisa decided that buying car paper might be a great way to invest a relatively small amount of money because these cars can be repossessed, which provides an opportunity to get a good return. To find out more, Lisa went to a "buy here/pay here" car business—basically, a used-car dealership.

This particular lot had about 70 cars and was located in Loveland, Colorado. It was owned by a guy named Tim, who bought cars from auto auctions for under $1,000 each, which he then sold to people for a down payment that usually equaled the total amount that Tim had paid for the car at the auto auction. Tim said that 90 percent of his customers paid with cash or money orders; they didn't even have a checking account. Tim financed the sales for a period of 2 or 2½ years at the highest rate allowable under Colorado usury laws. (Every state has different rates, so you need to check your local usury laws before you make any private loans or finance anything to anyone.)

Here's how it would work. Tim would go to an auto auction and buy a 1994 Honda for $400. He would then sell that Honda for $1,600, with $400 down. He broke even just with the down payment, so everything else he made was profit. Then he would finance the remaining $1,200 for two years at 21 percent interest, and his customer would make payments every month to Tim.

Tim didn't demand that his customers meet very stringent credit requirements. When Lisa asked him what type of prequalifications were required for someone to buy one of his cars, Tim replied, "They only have to answer two questions: Can they see lightning? And can they hear thunder? If they can answer those questions affirmatively, they get the car." In other words, Tim did not run credit checks on anyone. But that cut both ways. When Lisa asked what warranty Tim gave on his cars, Tim chuckled and said, "I guarantee that when they drive the car off the lot, the car is theirs, and if it breaks, that's just too bad."

His car sales included a $149 dealer prep fee. When Lisa asked Tim, "What does a buyer get for $149?" Tim said, "He gets the ability to buy the car." In other words, Tim is not the most ethical of businesspeople. Yet this is one of the fastest-growing businesses in the country right now.

Another way Tim made money was a result of the fact that 75 percent of his customers defaulted at some point, so Tim repossessed those cars. After he got a car back, he could sell it again for $1,600 with $400 down—all of which was profit since he had already earned back his initial $400 investment on the first customer who had defaulted. When Tim walked Lisa through his car lot to show her some of his not-so-fabulous cars, at least two cars on the lot had already been repossessed three times. So Tim had tripled his investment of $400 just on repossessed sales.

Lisa wasn't comfortable with Tim's business, but it was very interesting from a cash flow standpoint. This "buy here/pay here, tote-the-note" approach to selling cars is a growing industry. From an investor's standpoint, there are a couple of different ways to get into that type of business. Let's look at a few alternatives to Tim's approach.

Floor Plan Financing

Another way to invest is to *floor plan* a car, which means you put up money for people like Tim to attend auto auctions and buy cars in bulk, which obviously requires a lot of cash—a lot more than just $400 for one car. Tim secures your promissory note with the titles of the cars he buys with your money. As he sells each car and gets paid off, he in turn pays off your loan and releases the lien. You then give back the title to Tim, you get your money back, and that's the end of that deal. It's a very simple way to invest. You are basically making a loan—that is, a promissory note to Tim—that is secured by however many cars that you lend money to buy. And, of course, you earn interest on your loan to Tim.

Lisa did make a floor planning investment with another car dealer named Ken, who was based in Albuquerque and operated what was essentially a finance company. He bought car paper that was secured by dealers. Ken's special market niche was selling cars to people who lived on local American Indian reservations. He himself is not Native American; he simply had developed a relationship with the community near where he lives. The people who lived on the reservations had "buy here/pay here" cars that they had bought from local car dealers who had financed the purchases. Then Ken would buy the car paper (that is, the loans) at a discount. Lisa decided this was a good alternative investing opportunity, so she put up money for Ken to have the cash to buy this paper. Ken paid Lisa back at 15 percent interest for the length of the car loan, and Lisa's investment was secured by the car title.

If the car buyer didn't pay, Ken repossessed the car and then resold it, or he could do whatever he wanted with the car. That wasn't Lisa's problem because Ken was the person making payments to Lisa, not the person who had taken out the car loan. That's a very important distinction, and that's why Lisa felt comfortable making Ken the loan. More risk is involved when you make a loan to the person buying the car than when you buy car paper from an individual car dealer.

Lisa met Ken at an investors' conference, which, as we've noted, is how we find many of these alternative investing opportunities. As long as he was securing that car paper, Lisa was comfortable with this type of investment, even though the yield declined over time. Lisa started investing in Ken's business in 1997 with a $10,000 investment, but over the years, Ken reinvested her profits (instead of paying her interest) so that her initial $10,000 investment accumulated. In total, she probably has had about $25,000 invested in this business, and she has gotten a return of about 12 percent interest on average.

Although Lisa met Ken at a conference, she still did due diligence on him to make sure this was a good investment for her. Part of this due diligence was reading and verifying a prospectus that Ken provided, which included his credit history. Lisa further researched his business through the local chamber of commerce and the Better Business Bureau to make sure that Ken was a member in good standing. She also researched how long he had been in the paper business. She found out that Ken had been in the paper business secured by real estate before he got into the car loan business.

As mentioned, Ken's unique niche was working with people who lived on the American Indian reservations. He worked only with them because if someone on a reservation couldn't pay the loan, it was relatively easy to repossess that car because the tribal system would help out. In these cases, the tribal council gets back its own people's cars. In contrast, if you have to repossess a car, you first have to find the car, which can be very difficult and sometimes impossible. This made Lisa feel more comfortable in her investments. Another factor that increased Lisa's comfort level was that Ken was secured by the cars themselves, and he made copies of the titles for Lisa so that she could see what he was buying. Lisa also knew that she wasn't Ken's only investor. He probably had several hundred investors. In fact, his business was very successful because he had done very well in befriending and becoming the lender of choice for these American Indian reservations.

For those of you who are interested in investing in car paper, it's a very simple process. You go out and look for small buy here/pay here car dealers, and then you meet with them to ask the following questions:

- Where do you get the money to buy the paper at auction?
- Do you ever work with private investors?
- What would be my return if I were to put up some money for you to purchase automobiles?
- Could I try one or two deals and see how it works?
- Suppose I want to buy the loan after you sell the car to someone. What kind of yield would I make on that?
- What's my security for investing with you?
- Will I hold the original title to the car?
- How will I be paid back?
- Generally speaking, how long term are the loans you make?
- Do you get cash, checks, or money orders from your borrowers?

When investing with people who run a cash business like this, keep in mind that you don't know what income that business owner is really filing with the IRS. For example, when Lisa asked Tim about his accounting procedures, he told Lisa that the $50 and $100 bills went into one part of his wallet, and the $20s, $10s, and $5s went into another. Obviously, every business is supposed to report all the income and profit it makes, but you don't really know what someone is reporting to the IRS. Fortunately, it's not your responsibility to do due diligence on Tim.

Another positive benefit of floor planning is that you actually hold the title to the car because you have a trail of your investment, and how Tim collects his money from his borrower is none of your business. We think it's an interesting business, especially for individual investors who have only a small amount of money to invest and who want to buy something they can control, whether through your IRA or your personal investing accounts. Still, you need to understand there's some risk to this type of investment, just as with all investments. In many ways, this type of investment is similar to the check-cashing business, where people have to put up a check in advance to get money when they need it. There will always be people who need cash and can't get it through conventional means. Similarly, in the car business, most people need a car, but if they can't get credit from the conventional lending sources, where else are they going to go?

Providing Financing to People Who Need Loans to Buy Cars

Another way to invest in car paper is to lend money to the buyers of the cars, as Tim did. To do this, you create a note off the sale of these cars, which is, of course, a subprime loan because these car buyers can't get conventional bank financing since most of them have no credit. You, the investor, can buy the income stream from whatever dealer is selling the financing.

Recall our earlier example, where Tim paid $400 for a car he bought at an auto auction, then sold that car for $1,600 with a $400 down payment, and created a $1,200 note at 21 percent interest for two years. You could buy that income stream from Tim at a discount, which he might sell because he would rather have cash right now so that he can go out and buy more cars. For instance, you could pay Tim $800 for the right to receive $1,200 over two years from one of his customers. If that customer defaults on your car loan, you have two choices, depending on how you negotiate your deal. One option is for Tim to substitute the collateral — that is, the car that he will repossess from his customer — with another loan from another customer. In other words, Tim gives you another loan and takes that one back, which we feel is the best option. The other option is for you to repossess the car, but as investors, we don't really want to own a fleet of used cars, so that's not a good way to solve the problem of the defaulted loan.

You can profit by financing automobile notes because the subprime mortgage mess has created a large market of these buy here/pay here, tote-the-note used-car dealers. As of this writing, the used-car business is more popular than new-car dealerships due to the financial insolvency of GM and Chrysler, to name just two. In the past, used-car business owners got their financing to buy cars for resale from companies like American General Finance or other conventional finance companies, but now that source has dried up to some degree. So they're looking for private investors who are interested in making loans that are secured by used cars.

As we've said in all other chapters, *you need to do your due diligence* before you invest in car paper. In our opinion, the safest way to begin is to run a background check on the dealer. First find out how long the dealer has been in business. You might even consider running a Dun & Bradstreet check to know what the company's credit rating is. The number of years the dealer has been in business and the dealer's credibility are the most important factors. If you're going to buy notes, we think floor planning is the safer way to go because you're actually holding the titles to the cars that you've provided the funding for until they're sold.

Auto Pawning at Very High Interest Rates

Another way to buy car loans is called *auto pawning*. Unfortunately, this is another growing industry, and we're *not* recommending it as an investment; we're simply describing it for readers who may be interested. We have to admit that there are attractive aspects to auto pawning. First, the yields you can make are fantastic. Second, you get paid back very, very quickly. And third, you can invest with a very small amount of money that is secured by something tangible—in this case, cars, but it could also be notes, horse trailers, or anything.

Auto pawning works the same as pawning any other item. If somebody owns a car and then runs into a cash flow problem, that person can get a loan by pawning the vehicle. The people who auto pawn give their customers 50 percent of the worth of the car. The car owner has to put the car in a secured lot to receive the cash. When the car owner pays back the person or the company that's doing the pawning, the car owner also pays a very high interest rate—typically the highest the auto pawner can charge without violating the state usury laws.

If you're interested in auto pawning, you need to really understand the business because it is not for the faint of heart. It's not something we would ever invest in. With these types of investments—whether you're dealing in mobile homes, cars, horse trailers, cows, whatever—it's critical that you know what your state's usury laws are so that you don't charge above that interest rate.

How We Got Started Investing in Car Paper

Lisa had been a note buyer since 1988 in private mortgages secured by real estate. After doing that successfully for several years, she decided to investigate what other investments might generate similar cash flows. She started researching car loans because in the area of Colorado where she was living at that time, there were several dozen buy here/pay here, we-finance car people. She thought it would be very interesting to see how the car business worked and whether it might be a good investment for her.

After talking to a couple of local car lot owners, however, she decided that aspect of the car loan business wasn't right for her. She also wasn't interested in investing in the dealer preparation aspect of the business because there was no warranty on the cars they sold, and she didn't want to be involved in selling cars as is. If the car were to break down a week after someone bought it, the dealer wouldn't fix it. She felt this was taking advantage of people who needed a car and had no other choice but to buy one as is.

You may feel differently, however, so you need to decide what type of investment you're comfortable with. In Lisa's case, she preferred to invest in a safer aspect of car paper by floor planning a dealer or working with someone like Ken who ran that type of business. As with other investments, like real estate, there are many ways to invest in car paper. You simply need to decide what type appeals to you and what your investing goals are. Lisa based her choice on several factors. But the bottom line is that she trusted Ken because she did her due diligence on him—not only by researching his credit history and his business but also by looking at his actual operation. We've advocated throughout this book that a site visit is a good idea if you can do it: *go look at what you're investing your money in.* Lisa looked at Ken's operation in New Mexico, and he drove her around to several dealers that he did business with. Ken was very credible and ran a legitimate business, with a lot of people working for him and investing with him. All of those factors made Lisa comfortable investing with him, and those investments have paid off so well that she has continued to invest with him for almost 15 years.

INVESTING IN COWS (YES, COWS)

There are, of course, many other businesses you can invest in besides the car paper business. One of the most unusual we've come across is the cow business, which has evolved and changed over the years. You can invest in *cow paper* (that is, loans), where you invest in a creamery for dairy cows, using the actual cows as security for your investment. We ourselves have bought a cow contract. You can also invest in cattle herds used for beef production, but we haven't had any personal experience. But if you go online and research cattle, you will find many articles on this topic.

We started doing this in the mid-1990s. A creamery in the Midwest needed to raise funds, which we found out about through a broker who was also a CPA. He gave a presentation at an investors' meeting that we attended. He described an opportunity in which we could invest in a dairy cow for $6,779, and our investment was secured by an actual cow.

The paperwork on this type of investment is similar to a mortgage or a car loan, although there's no "title" to a cow. Each cow is given identification by the creamery, and you are supposedly secured by a particular cow, which you can go and see for yourself. We know investors who have done that as part of their due diligence. Moreover, you're further secured because if your particular cow dies, the creamery substitutes your collateral with another cow.

The creamery needs to use its cows as security for this type of loan because it typically has already pledged all its other equipment to the bank as security against its bank loans. Of course, the creamery needs to make sure that *all* its cows don't die or that it doesn't put up all its cows as collateral. But that's not likely to happen because this type of investment is typically made with a creamery that simply needs immediate cash flow. Which is why the interest rate is high, and the term of the investment is short.

Intermediaries, or brokers, represent the creameries and sell different types of loans that are needed to assist in running the operation. This is all private paper; you will not find it publicly traded. To find such brokers, you work through the Dairy Cattle Association. You're essentially investing in a creamery. Many creameries often need money to expand production but usually can't ask their bank for more money because they already have bank loans.

This type of alternative investment is similar to investing in a tenants-in-common arrangement. For example, it's like investing in a strip mall with a fractionalized interest. The mall has a master mortgage with some bank for $100 million, and then it takes a subordinated mortgage that you can invest in. You aren't in first position to get a return on your investment, but you are still putting up money toward this strip center mall. In this case, the creamery has a master mortgage with a bank, but it needs more money to produce its dairy products and to run its business. So the creamery utilizes private loans through intermediaries or brokers.

We no longer buy cow paper, but it certainly is an alternative investment opportunity that you might consider because it offers a tremendous yield. If you live in an area of the country where cows are a big part of the local economy, this type of investment might be something worth pursuing. If this is local to you, you can meet with the dairy farmers to learn more about their business and how they raise funds.

INVESTING IN PRIVATE REITs

Investing in private real estate investment trusts (REITs) is another option. Although these are real estate investments, we view them as business-to-business investments because you're investing in a trust rather than in a particular property. All REITs are secured by some form of real estate, whether it's a commercial strip center, an apartment building, or multifamily housing. There are several types of REITs: publicly traded, non-exchange-traded, and private. You can find out more about REITs by checking out the National Association of Real Estate Investment Trusts (NAREIT, www.nareit.com). Its Web site describes in further detail the differences between investing in the three types of REITs.

Publicly traded REITs are investments you can buy through a broker. They're essentially shares that trade on a national stock exchange and, as such, are regulated by the SEC. They're like mutual funds for real estate, and they're easy to invest in because they're liquid shares. If you have to sell them, it's not a big deal, although there is a transaction cost, of course. They're typically self-advised (just like stock mutual funds), so the managers of each fund do all the work to keep them together. The minimum investment in a publicly traded REIT is one share. Because they're regulated by the SEC, some people feel relatively safe investing in them because they have prospectuses and disclosures. However, investing in publicly traded REITs is not an alternative investment.

A *non-exchange-traded REIT* is also regulated by the SEC but, as the name of this type of REIT indicates, shares are not necessarily traded on a national stock exchange. Instead, you're buying individual shares through a third party. You must buy a minimum number of shares to invest this way. Because they're regulated by the SEC, non-exchange-traded REITs are required to make regular SEC disclosures, including their quarterly and yearly financial reports. The difference between these and publicly traded REITs is that there is no independent source of performance data for non-exchange-traded REITs as there is with publicly traded REITs. Another difference is that the typical minimum investment on a non-exchange-traded REIT is $1,000 to $2,500, depending on the particular REIT you're investing in. The returns are a little bit higher than on publicly traded REITs. That higher return depends on several factors:

- The type of REIT
- The term of the REIT
- The security for the REIT
- Whether it's a commercial REIT
- Whether it's a managed REIT

For more information on REITs that you can invest in, check out www.investmentinreits.com.

Because publicly traded REITs and non-exchange-traded REITs are not alternative investing opportunities, let's move on to the type of REIT that *is* an alternative to traditional investing: *private REITs.* Private REITs are secured by commercial buildings or other commercial real estate. Private REITs are not registered with the SEC, and their shares do not trade on national stock exchanges. As the name implies, they are private.

You can find people or companies that offer investments in private REITs on the Internet, through your local chamber of commerce, or through investing associations. Because they are run and managed by private companies or individuals, these investments pay a higher return. Typically, the investment starts at $1,000 and can go to $25,000. They're intended for individuals who can afford a higher minimum investment and who don't care about regulations or dealing with the SEC. Because the investments are not regulated by a government agency, they do carry more risk.

Private REITs are usually secured by major strip center malls or tenants-in-common. For example, Kohl's, the discount department store chain, is the largest REIT company. It offers publicly traded, non-exchange-traded, and private REITs. One benefit of a private REIT is that you're investing your money in a pool that's not secured by only one investment. You also need to understand that your return is going to be lower than owning individual properties because the risk is spread among multiple tenants. The only corporate governance over a private REIT is its own board of directors. Again, this is a private deal, so you don't have the same investor controls with this type of REIT as you would if you invested in the other two types.

In terms of due diligence, check with local attorneys to make sure that the REIT has been in existence for a while. You should also research public records to verify that it indeed has been in business for the time it says it has and that it has a good credit rating, a good Dun & Bradstreet rating, and a good Better Business Bureau rating. Your financial advisor or even your CPA should be able to help you find that out.

Private REITs are good investments for conservative investors who want to spread out their risk, aren't worried about making as large a return on their investment as they would with individual properties or other types of alternative investments, can afford to tie up their investing money for a longer period of time, and are willing to do due diligence on the management of that private REIT. The typical period of time that people invest in a REIT is five years, so that's how long your money will be tied up.

Making Loans to Businesses

Making loans to businesses is another way to earn interest on investments. To continue operating and be successful, every business needs to have cash readily available for such things as meeting its payroll, stocking inventory, and buying supplies and parts. Having the right credit in place is an important component of being successful, and many business owners need some way to obtain that credit. You can invest in businesses in many different ways. Let's look at some of these options individually.

Buying a Business's Accounts Receivable (aka Factoring)

Some businesses that run into financial problems factor their accounts receivables—they sell the revenue that is due to them in exchange for cash to cover their ongoing expenses. For example, suppose you are a crane operator working in construction. The city of Albuquerque is one of your clients, and you're working with a crew to fix the city's streets. Albuquerque is definitely going to pay you for your work, but they're not going to pay you in 30 or 60 days. Rather, it might take them as long as six months to pay you. In the current economy, it could take even longer if that particular city government is slow to pay.

Clearly, waiting for that money for work you've completed is challenging—your business has expenses of its own, and you need to maintain a healthy cash flow. This is why some businesses factor (that is, sell) that receivable that is due to them to a private investor or a financing company. The people who buy your receivables then advance you the money so that your business has the cash to make your payroll or for whatever you need to run your business. There are private investors and companies that specialize in factoring. As a business owner, if you become desperate for cash *now*, it is one way to get money fast.

To find businesses that are interested in selling their accounts receivable, one way is to contact your local city government and find out which projects the city is doing and the businesses they're working with. You could then contact those businesses to offer cash now for what they're owed by the city and will get eventually. You can also network through local chambers of commerce and check out your local business journals to find businesses that may be in need of immediate cash.

Lisa's personal experience with factoring involves a lawyer named Christina who has a small law practice with two attorneys and three staff members working for her. She needed $50,000 to buy a house, but she had no money. She was completely tapped out. Christina did have receivables: One of her clients was the city of Ocala, Florida. She was on retainer to the city, and she billed on a continual basis.

She approached Lisa about lending her money for her new house. Lisa agreed to make the $50,000 loan to Christina, which would be secured by those receivables. Therefore, if Christina did not pay Lisa back, Lisa could turn to the city of Ocala, and she would have the legal documentation to say, "Please send the money you owe to Christina to me instead." That security was better for Lisa than anything else Christina could offer as collateral. Because Lisa is not a lawyer, she wasn't interested in taking over Christina's firm. Pledging the receivables also worked for Christina because she knew the city would pay her *eventually*, so she would be able to pay Lisa back. The city was just not paying Christina fast enough for her to buy the house she wanted to buy *now*. And Lisa, as an investor, could help Christina with that—another win-win situation.

Making Small Business Loans

You can also make loans to businesses that need funds. There are two different ways you can make business loans. One is to lend money to someone who is selling their business. The business owner has found a buyer, but the only way the buyer can get financing to purchase the business is by taking back a seller-financed loan that the seller can sell to you, the investor. The security for these business loans is set up using a form called a Uniform Commercial Code document (UCC-1) that each state requires (which we also discussed in Chapter 2). The UCC-1 is the collateral instrument that you need to prepare when you are factoring or buying a business loan.

A second way is to make a private business loan to a business owner for whatever the need is—for example, the business might need cash to buy something, or maybe the business's bank loan is coming due and the business can't pay, which is not at all uncommon. According to the National Association of Realtors, more than $40 billion in commercial loans are coming due this year, and many of the businesses that took out those loans are not going to be able to come up with that balloon payment that is due to the bank. In fact, the residential real estate crisis that began with the subprime mortgage mess in 2008 might seem like nothing compared to what might be a huge depression in commercial loans that's likely to occur within the next few years. On the upside for investors, that situation creates a tremendous opportunity for those who are willing to lend money privately, and that investment is secured by the business itself.

How to Find Businesses That Need Small Loans

So how do you find businesses that need loans? One way is to check the business journals in your local area, which might have advertisements from companies that are being forced to put liens against different things. Another way is to work with local lenders or community banks who may have had to turn down a small business owner who came in for a loan, perhaps because the loan requested was simply too small for that lending institution—yet that fact might make that loan perfect for you as a private investor. You could establish a strategic alliance with that local lender, offering to talk to the people the lender or bank turns away. Many small banking institutions are not interested in making $35,000, $50,000, or even $100,000 loans. Instead, they're interested in making loans in the millions of dollars. So many small business owners are fallouts. They don't qualify, but not because they're bad credit risks or have a bad business model, but because the amount of money they want to borrow is just too small for these banks to bother with. In many cases, it costs just as much money to fund a $1 million deal as it does a $10,000 deal.

Lisa recognized this situation back in 1988, when she was living in North Carolina. She approached a local bank that had been bought out by a larger bank, which therefore changed the parameters of how it did business and at what level of loan. She asked the bank to refer to her any business owners that the bank turned away. She simply asked the bank to give those people her business card, especially those who were looking for loans of $50,000 or less. Lisa felt comfortable approaching this particular bank because she had a working relationship with them. But even if you don't know any bankers personally, you can ask your attorney or CPA or other professionals in your own network if they can introduce you to someone at the bank to pitch this idea in your market.

Although Lisa did this almost 20 years ago, it's still a viable way to make small loans today. After all, given the recent tightening of the lending markets, nobody has a crystal ball to determine whether banks will even consider giving people loans. The other issue is that many credit lines have dried up for people. The credit card companies are tightening their belts by lowering people's credit limits and shortening the float time because they're concerned they're not going to be paid back. For example, if you formerly paid your credit card bills on the 30th of each month, now your bill might be due on the 20th so that the company can get your money earlier. They might even raise your interest rate. People and businesses are very skittish, which results in real fallout for small business owners, because the lending guidelines that were good as recently as a year ago have changed. Many lenders are simply not making any deals. But that offers alternative investing opportunities for people like us.

In 1988, when Lisa first started making small loans to small businesses, the interest rates were pretty stable, but they were much higher than they are today. Yet banks were not making loans to small companies because they were more interested in the real estate business. The country had just come out of the savings and loan debacle, so there were no more little savings and loan institutions to make small loans. That created a situation in which people who needed to borrow $10,000 to $50,000 had no conventional lenders to turn to because the banks weren't willing to make that level of loan. But that price range is exactly the sweet spot for a private investor looking for alternative investing opportunities.

Here's an example of a small business that Lisa lent money to in 1988. Dave owned a small construction company that hired crane operators to work in mobile home communities. The crane operators would dig for new wells, septic systems, and sewers. Unfortunately, Dave failed to withhold payroll taxes for his crane operators and other employees, so the IRS imposed a fine and insisted that he pay it immediately or it would start garnishing his wages. Dave needed to sell some asset so he could pay off the IRS, so he sold an income stream of receivables for a very steep discount. Lisa put up $45,000 in three increments of $15,000 over the course of a year. This schedule enabled Dave to pay off the debt to the IRS without having to take a large amount of money from his regular account, and it meant that he could still operate his business.

As the investor in this type of deal, what you're trying to do (just as you do when you're buying real estate notes) is solve the person's problem. Of course, that solution needs to be an investment that is also worth your while. In this case, Lisa made 12½ percent interest on the investment. And everybody was happy: Dave was happy because he got the IRS off his back; the IRS was happy because it got paid and didn't have to garnish Dave's wages; and Lisa was happy because she earned 12½ percent interest on her investment.

Lisa worked through third parties, including accountants and mortgage brokers, who recommended her as someone who handled private financing. When she started getting calls, she printed up business cards that simply had her name and "Investor" or "Note Buyer" printed underneath. Today, you can't find small businesses that need loans this way because banks are so busy that they don't even have time to hand out your phone number. The best way of finding this type of alternative investing opportunity is by networking through business-to-business networks and contacting business brokers. You can also look in business journals, attend business classes and network with people attending those classes, or contact the local chambers of commerce.

We receive about one e-mail a month from somebody inquiring about the best way to go about getting a small loan. In this economy, many small businesses are finding that they simply can't get the money they need to stay in business because banks are cutting credit lines, have increasingly stringent compliance issues, are conducting more rigorous credit analysis, and auditing more financial statements. Businesses are having increasing difficulty in finding money to stay afloat. That's where *you* can help— and make money on your investment too.

Investing in Business Notes

We have a friend named Walter who specializes in buying business notes, specifically seller-financed notes. He buys business notes at about a 40 percent discount, for instance, on a $100,000 note, he pays $60,000.

For example, suppose someone—let's call her Mary—is interested in buying an American Speedy printing franchise. Mary has enough cash to make the down payment, but with the way the financial markets are right now, she can't get the rest of the financing to buy the franchise. In this situation, it might be possible for Mary to buy an existing franchise that is financed by the current owner, whom we'll call Diane. This is a common financing arrangement, and it would be subject to corporate approval because the business is a franchise.

However, Diane, who is selling the American Speedy franchise, also really needs cash. So Mary contacts Walter to see if he can help with any type of business financing. Walter has a few options in this scenario. He can lend Mary the money she needs to buy the American Speedy franchise, and he can charge her interest up to the allowable usury rate for the state that she's living in, which might be 18 to 20 percent. Or the seller, Diane, can create a note that Walter can buy at a discount, which he has offered to do.

One possible downside is that if Mary, who is buying the American Speedy franchise, does not keep the goodwill of the customers who have been bringing their business to Diane, Walter can lose his entire investment. That's the risk Walter takes. However, when Walter buys that American Speedy franchise seller-financed note at a discount, he is secured by the franchise agreement, by the lease, and by the equipment. If the business fails and if Walter has to put all the business's assets into a fire sale, he feels he can get enough money back that he will not get hurt on his investment. That's a very popular way to do business notes.

Lisa worked for Walter as a consultant for a year. During that year, all the yields on all of Walter's investments were much higher than conservative rates of return. When you buy notes at a discount, you're buying an income stream. For example, if you had a $10,000 note at 10 percent interest, Walter would buy that for $6,000, and his yield would be 20 percent or more—because of the time value of money, buying the note at a discount gives him the right to receive the income stream. Clearly, Walter makes out very well on these investments.

It's relatively easy to find this type of investment through business brokers. These brokers make their money only when they sell businesses. On average, these brokers take a 10 percent commission when they sell a business. If a business owner sells the business for $100,000, 10 percent of that goes to the business broker, which translates to a $10,000 incentive to look for some sort of creative financing to make the deal happen, for example, from a private lender. Brokers look for people like us who want to lend out money that is secured by a business. To secure your investment, you need to see a business plan and set up a repayment system, and you need to establish a fair interest rate and a short term for the loan.

The business plan should include an executive summary that provides at least the following information:

- How much money the business needs
- How long the business needs it
- How the business is going to pay it back
- The interest rate
- The exit strategy
- What happens if the business doesn't pay

In Walter's case with the seller-financed note, the note had already been created. He bought that existing paper at a steep discount because of the time value of money: After all, a dollar today is not going to be worth the same as a dollar 10 years from now.

Don't Lend Money to People Buying Businesses They Don't Really Know

It's really important to review someone's business plan before you invest in the business. However, sometimes even the business plan doesn't reveal the critical information you need to make a sound decision. And it's not always easy to assess a situation objectively until you learn as much as you possibly can about the deal and the new owner's plans.

Here's an example of a business loan Lisa advised an investor not to make because she didn't think it was a good investment. A successful, family-run Korean restaurant in Los Angeles was put up for sale by the longtime owners following the death of the father, who had been the principal manager of the restaurant. His widow did not want to keep the restaurant, and none of her children wanted to run it. She decided to sell it, but she wanted to sell it to another Korean because she had an emotional interest in keeping it as a Korean restaurant.

Running a restaurant is a difficult business, so if you want to succeed, you really need to know your business. This is not a business you can just buy and assume you'll continue to have the goodwill of the previous owner's customer base. Instead, what usually happens when somebody buys a restaurant is that things change. The menu changes, the cooking is not the same, especially if there's a new chef or a new staff, the new owners might raise the prices, or the customers might personally miss the previous owners.

Lisa's opinion was that this wasn't a good investment opportunity for several reasons. Although the new buyer was Korean and could speak Korean (which is how he found out about the sale—the previous owners had advertised it in a Korean-language newspaper), he did not know anything about the existing customer base or the Korean community in Los Angeles because he had never lived in L.A.—he was relocating from Chicago. He knew the restaurant business in his hometown of Chicago, but he wasn't familiar with the Los Angeles restaurant scene. That type of knowledge is an important factor: You need to know the local market to make a success of a restaurant under new management.

Because the prospective owner was Korean, spoke Korean, and had restaurant experience, the widow thought he was a good choice to whom to sell her business. The prospective owner could not get full financing to buy the business, so he needed to take out a business loan. However, he had no assets of any real value. Lisa advised the investor not to make the deal because there were too many uncertainties whether the new owner could maintain the previous success.

If you're investing in a business transition or if you're buying a business note where a new party has come in, *consider the goodwill factor.* Goodwill has a value, but what value does it have if you don't understand the market? The new owner needs to consider that as well for the business—as well as your investment in it—to be successful.

Know the Credit History of the Person to Whom You're Lending Money

It's surprising how many people don't check out the credit history of the people to whom they are lending money. To illustrate, here's an example of another investment opportunity that Walter was involved in, where one party got burned—but it wasn't Walter.

Walter was approached by the owner of an auto repair garage just outside of Las Vegas. The owner—we'll call him Carl—was an experienced and talented mechanic, but after 25 years in the business, Carl decided he wanted to sell his shop. He found a buyer willing to pay his $500,000 asking price, which included all the sophisticated equipment in the garage to facilitate repairs. Carl's business had a very good profit-and-loss statement, a great reputation in the community, and because Carl's shop had been in business for 25 years, the business had a strong base of loyal customers. The person who was buying Carl's business—we'll call him Mack—was a young, tattooed motorcycle guy, and he was very different from Carl. Mack offered Carl $250,000 up front—which certainly appealed to Carl—but he couldn't get financing for the other $250,000.

So Carl found Walter through an ad, which Walter runs in certain markets, that reads, "I Buy Business Notes for Cash." Carl called Walter and told him the situation: that he was selling his auto repair business, that he had been in business for 25 years, that he had found a buyer for the business (Mack) who had agreed to put down 50 percent in cash. Mack still needed 50 percent financing, so Carl wondered if Walter might be interested in investing in this deal.

Walter told Carl that he would make the deal provided that Mack checked out. He told Carl to take the 50 percent up front from Mack, create a loan (that is, a note) for the other 50 percent at 12 percent interest for 2½ years. Walter agreed to buy that note for the other $250,000, which he would buy from Carl for $125,000. With this deal, Carl would get $250,000 from Mack and another $125,000 from

Walter, which would be $375,000, *in cash*, today for his business. Carl thought that sounded great. Admittedly, he wasn't getting his $500,000 asking price, but he would be getting $375,000 in cash right away. Walter, of course, would get the other $250,000 that Mack would have owed to Carl, plus 12 percent interest over the next 2½ years.

It sounds like a good plan, right? Unfortunately, this example is a horror story, not a success story. As we've said throughout this book, part of financing business notes is *doing your due diligence*, and one party in this deal failed to do his. In this case, Walter's due diligence consisted of making sure that Carl's auto repair shop really existed and taking a look at the lease that Carl had signed to occupy the business because he needed to make sure that the lease was valid and had plenty of time left on the remaining term. Walter also needed to know a little bit about the credit history of the borrower because that was vitally important in assessing whether this was a good deal. He also ran a Dun & Bradstreet background check on Carl's business, and he made sure that the Better Business Bureau didn't have any complaints against the business. Finally, he made sure he understood what Carl (and Mack) needed the money for, and he made sure that Carl wasn't over his head in debt already. All of these are critical factors to check out before you do any type of lending.

Walter did extensive due diligence on Carl's business, but he wasn't so comfortable with Mack. In fact, he didn't trust him. Mack's credit wasn't the best, which Walter found out when he ran a credit report on him. Anybody who is selling a business should get an authorization from the prospective buyer to check that person's credit history to ensure that the buyer is creditworthy. You need to know what you're getting yourself into before you get into it. Walter knew that Mack wasn't an A+ credit-rated person—after all, if he had had A+ credit, Mack would have been able to get an SBA loan, and he wouldn't have needed Carl to try to get financing from Walter.

Because he thought Mack was a poor credit risk, Walter wasn't comfortable making the deal the way he had initially proposed it to Carl. Walter wasn't comfortable with Mack, but Carl thought selling to Mack was safe because Carl hadn't done enough due diligence on Mack. Walter restructured the deal to protect his interests. He told Carl, "OK, if you're vouching for Mack, let's put *your property* on the line." Walter had the presence of mind to attach a piece of land that Carl owned as other collateral on his loan to Carl because Mack didn't have any other collateral except his 50 percent down payment. Carl agreed to use that property as collateral, Carl sold his business to Mack, and Walter agreed to buy Carl's note.

Unfortunately, Walter received only one payment from Mack. Then a month to the day after the deal closed, Mack took everything he could from the garage, cleaned it out of all equipment, left the place vacant, folded up shop, and skipped town. That left Walter stuck with a garage with absolutely nothing he could even sell to try to recoup his $125,000 investment. But because Walter had done his due diligence and had structured the deal with Carl to protect himself, when Mack went into the wind, he left Carl, not Walter, on the hook because Carl had agreed to put up some of his property as collateral. So Walter could then take Carl's land. If Walter had found any equipment or parts or *anything* left in the garage that he could have sold to get at least some of his money back, he would have done that.

One recourse for Carl would have been to write off this loss if his tax situation allowed it, and that might have been the best thing Carl could do. We don't know what Carl did; all we know is that Walter protected himself. If he hadn't attached collateral, Walter would have been out $125,000. Of course, Walter could have gone after Mack, but Walter would have had to hire a private investigator to try to find him, which is no easy thing to do. Mack had probably already sold the equipment (which he essentially stole from Carl) on the black market. Plain and simple, Mack scammed Carl. Unfortunately, Carl didn't do enough due diligence on Mack to protect himself.

If you are thin-skinned or risk averse, investing in business notes can be very scary. One way to protect yourself is to make sure that the borrower has a business plan. If you're not comfortable, you can ask the borrower to put six months of payments in an escrow account. If the borrower doesn't pay, at least you have some of the payments. Also, have an attorney draw up the paperwork to protect your interest in any type of business dealings. So when investing in business notes, protect yourself by reviewing the business plan, setting up an escrow account, and having your lawyer draw up the agreement.

How to Structure a Loan If There's No Tangible Collateral

Investing in business notes is different from private lending. The difference lies in the security for the loan. For example, suppose you know a caterer—we'll call her Rita—who's just terrific. She works with her sister Estelle, and they make fabulous food that is served beautifully. Rita wants to expand her business because she has so many people who want to hire her that she can't handle all the business she's getting. She wants to hire a few assistants to help her cook and bake, more staff to help her serve, and other profession-als, including a bookkeeper-accountant and maybe even a marketing or PR person to help promote her business even more widely than the great word-of-mouth recommenda-tions she's already getting.

But Rita can't get a loan because her business doesn't have a continuity of clients. She specializes in big parties and weddings, which obviously most clients don't have all the time. And she really doesn't have any security for that loan. What has the most value in Rita's business is her own skill, talent, and reputation as a terrific caterer. Because the lending market is very tight right now, what can Rita do? She can look for a private investor who believes in her busi-ness because Rita has over 20 years experience cooking for various restaurants in her area, she's very well known among foodies, and she knows many companies who refer Rita and her business to people who need a caterer. Also, Rita has a business plan, but she needs to beef it up so that potential investors can understand what she really does. What is the value of Rita's business? That's the first thing that you, the investor, need to look at.

The value of Rita's business is the *referral system* that she has with some key related businesses (for example, florists, party venues, formal dress shops, and invitation printers). Rita is known for her creativity in planning menus. She's known for her skill in preparing a wide variety of delicious food (no matter how unusual or simple: even her meatloaf is to-die-for yummy). She's known for being unflappable, calm, and a pleasure to work with. That's important to people who are hosting large parties—like weddings—and want to make sure that every detail is perfect so that their guests will thoroughly enjoy themselves and the event will be memorable. She's known for continuing to attract new clients because of her stellar reputation. She has great goodwill, and she has recently developed a Web site to provide further credibility for her business and to include testimonials from previous clients who were delighted with her work. So what an investor is buying in this case is *Rita* and her ability to continue to grow her business. Nevertheless, the investor who is considering lending her money needs to have some sort of security for that loan.

What could Rita offer as security for a loan? If Rita has six or seven clients lined up who have already agreed to pay her $10,000 per event, and if that income stream is going to come in regularly every month, Rita could assign some of her receivables to an investor in lieu of a loan. After all, when Rita (or any small business person in any type of business) sends a client an invoice, she has the money that she owes to you. If a client has to pay the $10,000 over five installments, that would bring in $2,000 a month. Rita could assign to you $1,000 of that $2,000—leaving herself $1,000 so she would not be crippling herself to you (her investor) in the course of paying back the loan over the five-month period. That's one way Rita can structure the deal.

However, you (the investor) want to protect yourself the best you can. This is actually an unsecured loan because there really is no security. This is an intangible business because, again, the security is Rita. Still, many investors will make a loan like this one because they look at Rita's business and decide, "OK, I know Rita. She's got a great history. I spoke to three of her previous clients, and they all believe in her ability to do a great job. They send her business. I feel it's a pretty safe loan." The investor—that is, *you*—has to make that decision. You've got to do your due diligence on Rita's business to make sure it's legitimate. Does she really have contracts with clients lined up? Is she getting continual monthly income? Is she a good credit risk? What's the worst that can happen? Those are the questions an investor needs to ask.

You can find alternative investing opportunities like Rita's business primarily through word of mouth and by networking. For example, one of Rita's clients might know that she wants to expand her business and needs some money. You, as the investor, need to make some interest on your money, so you find out how much cash Rita needs, and then you decide how much you need to receive so that you will feel comfortable with this type of alternative small business investment. This type of deal is a truly custom-negotiated deal, because Rita doesn't have a tangible business in the way that Carl the auto mechanic or Dave the construction company owner had. So you need to decide what's right for *you* in this investment and any investment you make — whether it's a traditional investment or an alternative investment like those we're describing in this book.

Don't Lend Money to Businesses You Don't Believe In

For whatever reason, investors often make the mistake of investing in something they don't think will work. Before you invest in anything, review the business plan and consider whether you think the business is viable. Ray, an HR professional by day, also loved comic books. In his spare time, he was trying to get into the business of brokering ads in comic books. With this type of business, Ray wouldn't get paid until the ad was placed in a magazine, but he believed he had the contacts and the desire to make this business work. He was confident that he could make a six-figure income selling ad space in comic books. Unfortunately, Ray had no money. For him to get out there and try to bring together the comic book with the advertiser, Ray needed some cash.

Ray lived in California, but the annual comic book convention was in Chicago. He knew he needed to go to that convention to meet with publishers face-to-face and convince them to include ads in their comic books. He needed to meet with the right potential advertisers—companies whose products would appeal to comic book readers. He had no money to cover his travel expenses, and he needed seed money to launch his business and get it off the ground. Ray approached Lisa because he knew she was always looking for alternative investing opportunities. Of course, the first question Lisa asked him was, "Where's your business plan?"

Ray came back to Lisa with a plan for his business. When she reviewed his plan, however, it was clear that he wanted to create an entire company and delegate all the responsibilities of the actual business development to someone else. Because of that, Lisa decided not to invest in his business since Ray himself had no personal vested interest. Ray was not going to actually sell the ads. Instead, he wanted to get financing for his business idea and then hire a salesperson on commission to sell ad space in the comic books.

The point of this example is that Lisa didn't turn down the deal until she reviewed the business plan. If you're interested in making private business loans, you have to know what you're getting into. No matter how well you think you know someone or how much you trust the person, you have to develop an attitude in your mind that says "trust but verify." That's exactly what the people who turned their hard-earned life savings over to Bernie Madoff should have done. Every one of Madoff's clients simply *believed* in him—they all thought he would take good care of them—yet he ran off with their money. So do your due diligence. We cannot emphasize this caveat enough. In fact, that's one thing we love about alternative investing: It forces investors to think about what they are investing in before they write the check.

Should You Invest in an Experienced Businessperson's New Business?

Here's another example of a businessperson who was seeking investment money in a new business. Eddie was someone Lisa knew as a very active note buyer. He had been buying seller-financed mortgages at a discount as a business for many years. A few years ago, Eddie decided to expand his horizons and start teaching his business concept to others. He developed a business called The Note School, which was intended to provide education and mentoring to people who wanted to learn how to invest in seller-financed notes that were secured by residential real estate. Eddie connected with an infomercial guru, he developed his speaking and teaching skills, and he started going around the country speaking professionally about his area of expertise.

Eddie's goal in this new business venture was to teach people how to find these deals, at which point they would bring the deals to him. He would do all the due diligence, and then he would be the broker in the middle and sell the deals to funding sources. Unfortunately (as we all now know), the real estate market changed because of the subprime mess and the tightening in the lending arena, so very few lenders were offering private seller-financed mortgages anymore. The lenders had become extremely cautious because too many buyers had obtained seller-financed mortgages two years earlier when interest rates were low and anybody could get a loan and didn't pay them back.

Eddie's new business was going really well, but then the borrowing scene changed and there were no funding sources to tap. He found himself in a situation in which people didn't see an opportunity in his teaching them to be bird dogs to find new investing opportunities from seller-financed mortgages. So he needed a new way to continue to support himself. He decided to try to develop other alliances and work with other types of cash flows and develop a school for all alternative cash flow investing. He wrote a business plan that described how he would do that.

In Eddie's favor, he had a history of being successful with The Note School. In addition, he had put together some products, including books, tapes, and DVDs, that he could sell and would be a profit center. He also started working with some associations to get his foot in the door and capitalize on the concept of teaching people to become self-sufficient in money matters and become entrepreneurs in the alternative cash flow industry. With all this as background, Eddie approached Lisa and asked if she would like to be a funding source for him if he were to get this new business off the ground. And Lisa would because Eddie has 25 years' experience in the business, and he is a very well connected, honest, and ethical person.

But if he were to approach *you* to invest in his business, and you didn't know all this, you would need to decide whether you were interested in making him a private loan. How would you know if he's honest? Is this somebody you've known for a long time? *You* have to decide if you're willing to take that risk. After all, Bernie Madoff had 25 or more years of experience in his business, and his clients believed that he was knowledgeable, successful, honest, and ethical—until he confessed that his business was just a giant Ponzi scheme, and he had defrauded all the people who gave him money to "invest," which he spent instead of investing. Just as with Bernie Madoff's business, if you decide to invest in Eddie's business, that investment is unsecured because he has no collateral (just as Bernie Madoff had no collateral).

Whether to invest in Eddie's new business is really the same as deciding whether to invest in Rita's catering business because it's an intangible business, and the only collateral is Eddie himself. If Lisa believed enough in Eddie's idea, and if she thought his business plan was strong enough, and if the term of the money that Eddie needed and that Lisa invested was short enough, Lisa would consider investing in his business. She would use her IRA because she doesn't need her IRA money right now. She wouldn't invest any of her personal money if she needed to live on it because for her the investment is too risky.

INVESTING IN START-UP BANKS

Another alternative investing opportunity related to cash flow is start-up banks, also called *de novo banks*. In many parts of the country, groups of people are getting together to organize a community-based bank. Each state sets a certain dollar amount that the bank's founders need to have to get a charter to start a community bank.

Lisa has made this type of alternative investment too. Almost three years ago, Lisa invested through her IRA in a new start-up bank in San Francisco. The founders raised the minimum capital requirements, their prospectuses were approved by the SEC, and the bank now has four branch offices in the

San Francisco Bay Area. As of this writing, Lisa has not seen one dime of a return on her investment. But she's not worried, because this is an investment that does not pay monthly, quarterly, or annually. Instead, it will make money when the bank either sells off to another institution or it becomes sufficiently profitable to be able to start paying dividends.

Lisa found out about this investing opportunity when she attended a local chamber of commerce event where the person who is now the CEO of the bank was speaking about it. He mentioned that he was going to have a separate meeting for those who were interested in learning more of his plans, so Lisa went to that event too. She thought it was an interesting idea, and the CEO presented a very well organized plan. The senior management had strong, extensive experience working for some of the country's biggest banks—including First Republic (which is now owned by Bank of America) and Wells Fargo. His plan and his management team were two strong factors that persuaded Lisa to invest in this new bank.

Another factor that appealed to Lisa was that the other investors in this bank were people who owned 28 well-known national franchises. One investor was the owner of the largest venture capital company in the San Francisco Bay Area. These people really understood markets, so Lisa felt comfortable investing some of her IRA money in this startup bank. She wanted to know who the other investors were. To find out, she had to sign legal disclosures. The final factor that convinced Lisa to invest was the type of loans that the bank was making. It was not going to make any residential real estate loans at all. Instead, it was going to make only commercial loans to businesses.

This start-up was founded before the subprime mortgage mess, yet its lending practices were very careful. Lisa felt even more fortunate that its business model anticipated what eventually happened in the economy. Overall, Lisa felt comfortable with the professional and business background of the investors, the business plan, the founders' years of experience in banking, and the locations of the banks that they planned to set up. Lisa feels this is a very safe investment that will eventually earn about a 25 percent return each year, and the time frame she's looking at is about five years.

Keep in mind, however, that this type of alternative investment is tricky because when you invest in start-ups or private placements, you truly are rolling the dice. You're believing in what you're seeing. You're saying to yourself, "I believe in the concept. I believe in the product. The company seems to have a good business plan. The executive in charge seems to have experience in the industry. I feel secure in the nature of the business, and the prognosis for its future. It's a business that's relevant and timely in today's marketplace." These are factors that you, as an alternative investor, need to take into consideration before you decide to go forward.

The private lending industry is growing. People who have money—whether it's personally or in their IRAs—will see that it's easier and easier to find these alternative investing opportunities because the traditional lending markets have tightened up. But remember, if *you're* the bank, you need to be the bank and *do your due diligence*!

Investing in Equipment Leasing

Equipment leasing is another way to develop a cash flow, but instead of owning a note secured by something, your investment is secured by a lease. Equipment leasing is basically a loan in which the lender (again, in this case, a private lender—that is, you) buys and owns the equipment, and then rents it out to a business at a flat monthly rate for a specific number of months. Or you can be the middle person and assign payments.

If you own the equipment, at the end of the lease, the business that has been renting the equipment from you can purchase it at fair market value or for a fixed predetermined amount. The business can also just continue leasing the equipment or choose to return it. This is similar to leasing a car. For example, if Honda is the lessor and you are the lessee, you might lease a car for three years. At the end of those three years, you can either buy the car or you can return it back to Honda. You can do the same with any other equipment. You, the lender-lessor, own the equipment, and you can lease it to somebody who needs it.

For instance, you could buy a very good copier machine for $10,000 and then lease it to a small company. That company doesn't have $10,000 to buy a copier, but it needs a copier on site. So it leases it from you and makes lease payments to you. And even if *you* don't have the $10,000 to buy the copier and lease it out, you can buy the equipment on a payment-installment basis and then sublet it to a small business. You just need to make sure that the small business (which is the lessee) makes its payments to you and that you make a spread.

We know a few investors who have made this type of investment, not with office equipment but with cars. Typically, they hear of someone who needs a car but doesn't have the money to buy one, which the investors usually find out by word of mouth. For example, maybe you know someone, such as a college student, who needs a car. You could buy a $10,000 used Saturn. You hold the title to the car, but the college student makes the payments of, say, $200 a month until the car is paid off. In that scenario, you could earn 12 percent interest on your investment in this car, while the college student makes the payments. And if the student doesn't pay off the car, you get to take the car back.

As mentioned, this type of arrangement is typically found through word of mouth. To find this type of deal, you simply need to keep your ear to the ground and have a wide network, so you can connect with someone who needs some type of equipment. Many small companies cannot afford to buy a good copier, but realize that they're spending $300 to $400 a month at Kinko's to make copies. If they can find an investor who's willing to buy the copier up front and then they can repay the investor with interest, that approach works for both parties.

Another example of this type of leasing is the rent-to-own furniture and staging industry. These companies make a fortune by renting out their furniture to homes that are on the market and need to be staged to make a better impression on potential buyers. We would definitely lend money to those businesses because that type of investment makes you money while you sleep. The only other factor to consider in this type of arrangement is what you will do if your lessee defaults on your loan and you're stuck with the equipment, the car, the furniture, or whatever you're leasing. Whenever you lend money to others—even if it's a family member or friend—you need to be careful and you need to think about what your recourse will be if that person doesn't pay you back. For example, if you buy a car for your son under an agreement that he will make the payments, and he stops making his payments, what can you do? Are you going to repossess his car? Probably not.

In many cases, it's better to make loans that are not personal. As Shakespeare said, "Neither a borrower nor a lender be," and that's certainly true when it comes to friends and family. But if you're making a loan as a business deal, it's not personal, and you don't have the same concerns about what to do if you're not paid back.

Alternative investments, private lending, and notes secured by a business make sense under the right circumstances for investors who understand the business, its purpose, and its exit strategy should there come a time when it needs one. Again, this is not an investment approach for everyone, but in today's tough financial world, the investor who has the cash gets to choose!

CHAPTER

9

MAKING ALTERNATIVE INVESTMENTS VIA YOUR IRA OR 401(k)

All of the alternative investments we've described in this book can be made through your IRA or 401(k). People have been able to make alternative investments using IRA and qualified plan funds since 1975. However, a remarkably small percentage of taxpayers use their IRAs and 401(k)s and other qualified plans to invest in alternatives to the usual stocks, bonds, mutual funds, and certificates of deposit (CDs). In fact, of all the trillions of dollars presently in retirement plans and IRAs, only 1.5 percent are being invested in real estate, notes, private placements, gold, and the many other investments available.

A BRIEF HISTORY OF INVESTING VIA IRAs

We first discovered how to invest in alternative investments through an IRA or 401(k)[1] back in 1979. Hugh was working

---

[1] At the time, these retirement accounts weren't even 401(k)s. They were Keoghs or HR 10s, but because those accounts have become 401(k)s, we refer to them as 401(k)s for simplicity.

as the general auditor for a multibank holding company in California, and he discovered that the company's trust division was handling self-directed IRAs. Some of the company's clients weren't simply investing their IRAs in CDs; they were investing in real estate as well as small companies, which were then called limited liability partnerships (LLPs). (LLPs are now usually limited liability corporations, or LLCs; the LLP structure isn't used by many organizations today.)

Hugh found it interesting that people were investing in something other than a safe and secure investment, such as an FDIC-insured CD. These individuals were instead doing things like investing in tracts of land in the California desert, developing that land, and making a huge amount of money. Some clients were developing properties in Mexico for the tourist trade, which was even more intriguing.

Over the next few years, Hugh left that multibank holding company and started consulting in bank operations, mergers, and acquisitions. But he remained in contact with one of the administrators who was overseeing these much more interesting alternative investments. As time went on, this practice of investing in alternatives through an IRA or 401(k) became so familiar to us, so we assumed that everybody did it and that it wasn't rare at all. But we discovered that wasn't true.

This was before investing in mutual funds really became commonplace, which was in 1985 or so. Before the mid-1980s, the stock market was something that only wealthy people invested in by buying blue-chip stocks in individual companies like IBM or AT&T. Average middle-class people didn't invest that way; instead, they saved their money in savings accounts, or they bought a little real estate (such as a rental property or two), or they bought government bonds or T-bills. After mutual funds came into play, however, our clients invested in them, but they also became interested in investing their IRA and 401(k) funds in alternatives such as real estate, and those alternative investments became the mainstay of our business.

Meanwhile, very few people were investing in undeveloped land in California and Mexico (or anywhere), which was the investing approach that had originally intrigued us back in 1979. Because those investors were so few and far between, information about how this was done was confined to upper-level investors—investors who typically had $100,000 to $200,000 in their retirement accounts, which was a lot of money back then. (Upper-level investors today tend to be in the range of $250,000 and up.) We got to know these higher-level investors because we would give lectures to them. As a matter of fact, there were so few of this type of investor that we knew every one of our clients personally until about four to five years ago. When one of our clients was interested in investing in something new— whether it was undeveloped land, oil and gas exploration, solar power, or gold—we worked together to figure out how to make these deals. Because they were so unusual at the time, we needed to make sure that they were legal and that we weren't making any prohibited transactions.

BUYING LAND VIA AN IRA

The first clients we had who wanted to use their retirement accounts to invest in alternative investments were two former insurance agents who wanted to invest in real estate.

The IRAs that they had with their insurance company allowed them true self-direction, basically allowing them to invest in pretty much anything. IRAs are much more fluid investment vehicles than most people realize because the investment possibilities are usually prescribed by the IRA custodian. Because most custodians are banks or brokerage houses, the investment options are limited to what they offer. If you have your IRA with a custodian that permits true self-direction, you can invest your IRA in any of the investments mentioned in this book.

Our clients invested in land in Lancaster and Palmdale, California, about 70 miles north of Los Angeles near Edwards Air Force Base. Lancaster first attracted residents in the 1970s, but then it started booming in the 1980s. But when these investors started buying land in this area, there wasn't much there. They got together with a few others and bought large tracts of land. They subdivided that land into parcels that could be developed for housing for the people who worked at the air force base and its support activities out there. Some of the investors subdivided the land themselves and sold the properties, some sold the land to someone else who developed it, and some formed joint ventures with people who developed the land.

They all made a pile of money because, in 1979, a 10-acre tract of land out in the California desert probably cost between $1,000 and $5,000 an acre. A couple of those investors are still clients of ours, and they had about $1 million in their accounts from those land investments after only about five years. Clearly, these were phenomenal investments, and to add to the deal, the investments were tax deferred because they were made through their retirement accounts.

Buying Land outside the United States via an IRA

Some of these clients also wanted to buy and develop land in Ensenada, which is in the Mexican state of Baja California. They visited there and tried to acquire beachfront property. At first, they thought this would be as easy as buying land in California, but it turned out not to be because at that time it wasn't easy to buy real estate as a foreigner. In Mexico, you can't simply buy a piece of property. Property is held in a trust by a bank in Mexico. So you (or your IRA) actually buy into an LLC, which has a security interest in that trust in the bank in Mexico.

Many Americans and other non-Mexicans didn't know this, however. So what often happened is that someone would visit Mexico and attend a condo development meeting to attract potential real estate buyers. These meetings were often held on the beach, where it was beautiful and warm and the breezes were terrific. The potential buyers would drink too many margaritas, and that's when the real estate agent would say, "Hey, for you, I have a special deal. Wouldn't you like to own the condo that you're staying in right now?" If they had the money to do that, many people would often readily agree, which was when the agent would say, "That's great, just sign here."

But it wasn't and isn't that simple, unfortunately, and many investors found that out the hard way and got burned. As we researched how to make these investments, we found that real estate agents in other countries often try to sell other people's interests in a property. For example, suppose someone like the condo buyer we just described—let's call him John—bought a property and then regretted buying it.

So John decides to sell the property. The real estate agent then tries to sell John's security interest to someone else—let's call her Susie—and the agent reassures Susie that John can simply convey his interest to her. But property transfer doesn't work that way in Mexico. Instead, John needs to relinquish his interest in the trust, and Susie has to start over again, going through the bank and doing the same thing John had to do when he bought the property. Unlike the United States, John cannot simply sell the ownership of his house to Susie. So if you're investing in international real estate, *you need to know about the local laws* to ensure that your transaction is legal and your investment is protected.

The investment works the same way if the investor is buying the property through her IRA or 401(k) because then the IRA (or any other retirement account) acts as the surrogate for the person who's buying the property. The IRA in the United States purchases that interest through a corporation, so if you're interested in buying foreign real estate, all you need to do is direct your IRA custodian regarding what you want to do.

Unfortunately, as mentioned, the people who invested in Mexico early on got burned because they didn't make those transactions properly in accordance with Mexican laws. Those laws also stipulated that a foreign national could not own property within 50 miles of the seashore. Of course, beachfront locations were exactly where the investors wanted to buy. To get around that law, some U.S. investors decided to partner with a Mexican national, who would act as the U.S. buyer's surrogate. When the Mexican authorities discovered that people were doing that, they took back the property from the U.S. "owners"—which meant that those buyers lost their land and lost the money they had invested in it. That Mexican law has since been modified, so there is more freedom today regarding *where* foreigners can buy property in Mexico. But the laws regarding *how* foreigners can buy property still mandate that the sales must be made through a master trust account with a Mexican bank.

Property Ownership Laws outside the United States

When investing in other countries, keep in mind that each country has its own laws and regulations—and it can be complicated. And investing via your retirement funds adds another layer. For example, we have clients who are from India but live in the United States. They want to invest in property in India because it is very inexpensive, and people who develop land can make a good amount of money if they know what they're doing. Unfortunately, there's one problem: You cannot purchase property in India via an IRA or trust account. Indian law does not permit a U.S. IRA—in other words, a foreign entity—to own property in India.

Indian law *does* allow *individuals* who are Indian nationals, regardless of what citizenship they hold, to own property in India. Furthermore, under certain circumstances, an Indian corporation can own property. Investors who want to buy property in India via an IRA must form an Indian corporation, at which point their IRA or 401(k) can take an interest in that Indian corporation and then acquire property.

Obviously, it's not practical for the average investor—or even for a very sophisticated investor—to know the laws of every country in the world. If you do want to invest in foreign countries, you need to be sure you're abiding by the local laws so that you don't buy foreign real estate only to find that your purchase was illegal and the country's government is confiscating your property and keeping your money. If you want to invest in alternative investments—whether it's real estate or anything else—you need to find someone who *does* know the laws pertaining to investing in the country you're interested in.

Entrust has established relationships with banks in other countries because that's the only way we can do business in those countries for our IRA or 401(k) clients. If a client approaches Entrust about buying property in another country, we can facilitate that investment via a local bank. It's best to make these investments through a company that is not only based in the United States but has experience making these transactions because it's difficult for individual investors—no matter how savvy they are—to figure out how to do this on their own. We know many people who have made these deals incorrectly.

When you're investing via your IRA, the asset you buy must be vested in the IRA. Some people have acquired assets in other countries, only to find out later that they had vested in their own personal name, not in their IRA. Under U.S. tax law, that's illegal and it is a prohibited transaction. Those investors could lose their entire IRA, *all of it*, even the assets that aren't part of the real property or were bought correctly. The laws are draconian. You might think, "Well, okay, I'll just buy this property, and if I lose it, no big deal." That's not the case at all: *you risk losing your entire IRA* because the U.S. government doesn't want you to make any prohibited transactions, and this is their punitive approach to preventing them.

You have to look carefully to find qualified and experienced professionals or investing companies in the United States that can help you buy alternative investments via your IRA or 401(k). Let's say you're fluent in Italian. You go to Italy and find a beautiful little town in Tuscany like Orvieto or Siena, and you decide that you want to buy property—either to run as a bed-and-breakfast or as some other type of rental property. Or perhaps you want to buy a vacation home for yourself. Even if you research all the Web sites we've suggested in Exhibit 6.2 as well as local Web sites specific to buying property in Italy, you can't then just call up Schwab or Fidelity or Vanguard or some other company that you typically invest through to handle that foreign real estate investment. The typical agent at the typical investment company will probably just give you a glazed-over look because he or she doesn't make those types of transactions.

Instead, you need to contact a company—like Entrust— that has been helping their clients buy alternative investments and is thoroughly familiar with what is involved. Entrust has enormous experience in handling myriad complex transactions. The types of questions that we ask include, "Where's the property that you want to buy?" "Who's our contact person in Orvieto? Who's the attorney who will handle the deal? Who's the notary?" We would then contact all those individuals and handle the investment transaction for you. The key to international investing is having a bank-to-bank relationship, as well as knowing all the laws that are relevant to the specific transaction and investment that interests you. And like the United States, those laws can change, so you need to make sure you have current information.

CHAPTER

10

WRAPPING UP

What we have tried to do throughout this book is to give you the tools necessary to make informed choices on alternative investments that may fit into your portfolio. From real estate, cows, and businesses to gold, oil, energy, and more, there truly is a world of choices for investors who want to go beyond the stock market, for investors who don't want others to vote on their money, and for investors who want to be directly involved in keeping the money they have worked so hard to accumulate for their retirement and their life savings. Are you that type of investor?

No one can really determine what is going to happen in the market next month, let alone next year. Will there be Social Security when we retire? What will be the state of the banking industry? Will foreclosures worsen and property values continue to fall?

We believe that the answers to those questions do not matter. Because when you are the type of investor who wants to control your financial portfolio, you will stay the course, you'll have a plan you can modify as you see fit for your needs, and you will invest based on that plan. So it does not matter what all the financial gurus, advisors, or economists have to say. Instead, all that matters is what *you* think!

Welcome to the society of those who have finally said, "No more!" Who have said, "It is up to me. I will take control of my financial future and let the cards fall where they may. I may not win every time, but at least I will make the decisions about how to invest my own money."

Lisa recently attended the World Money Show, where more than half of the people attending had lost more than 50 percent of a portfolio that they could not afford to lose. It hurt! Many had lost even more in their 401(k) plans. Those who admitted these losses said that they had had enough!

We wish to leave you with a final sad but true story. Sheila was 78 years old. She was widowed in 1979, and she inherited a business and a bank account that in today's dollars would be worth more than a million dollars. She knew nothing about business, so over the years, she proceeded to run the business into the ground. She had Keogh plans [the former name for 401(k) plans] and cash, but she spent her way down to her last $250,000. At that point, 12 years ago, she finally woke up.

She hired a financial advisor to control her money. First he invested her money in junk bonds (which was the worst thing he could have done for her because she was in the 15 percent tax bracket). Then he sold those and put a third of the money in an annuity where he got a 9 percent commission, put another third of the money in stocks (she was age 65 at the time), and left the rest in cash.

By the time she turned 78, Sheila was just about broke. She did not disclose how much money she had left—not even to her accountant. But we know that she recently called her oldest daughter with a proposition: would her daughter consider buying a condo that the daughter would own but that Sheila could live in until she dies, at which point the daughter could take it over. Her daughter was in shock. Sheila finally admitted that she was not sure she had enough money to continue to make her rent payments. She confessed that she stayed up at night and worried, her eyes glued to CNN to see if the market was coming back. She hoped for a rebound so she could make up the monthly difference that she was then taking out of the little principal she had left.

Don't let this happen to you or any of your family members. Don't become another casualty of the current economy. When the Depression hit in the 1930s, what survived? Hard assets, real estate, gold, and commodities. That could again be our future. You don't have to agree with us. We are not financial wizards, we are not brokers, we do not have a securities license, and we do not tell people how to invest their money. Our goal is simply not to become or to know someone who is in the same financial straits as Sheila.

We wish you all the best in your investing and in your choice for financial freedom!

INDEX

ABOUT THE AUTHORS

Hubert Bromma is the founder and CEO of The Entrust Group with headquarters in San Francisco. A leading authority on the diversification of assets in tax-free and tax-deferred environments, he has written several books and appears frequently on television and radio financial programs.

Lisa Moren Bromma has 30 years' investing experience, primarily in real estate and in the cash flow industry. She is the author of *Wise Women Invest in Real Estate* and *Real Estate Investing for the Utterly Confused* and the editor of *Wise Women Investor*.